ISLAMIC BUSINESS ETHICS

Rafik Issa Beekun

International Institute of Islamic Thought
Herndon, Virginia, U.S.A.
1417/1997

Human Development Series No. 2

The International Institute of Islamic Thought
580 Herndon Pky., Suite 500
Herndon, VA 20170-5225 USA
Tel: (703) 471-1133 Fax: (703) 471-3922 E-mail: iiit@iiit.org

Library of Congress Cataloging-in-Publication Data

Beekun, Rafik Issa
Islamic Business Ethics / Rafik Issa Beekun

p. 88 cm. 23 — (Human Development Series ; 2)
Includes indexes
ISBN 1-56564-242-2
1. Business ethics 2. Islamic ethics
3. Management -- Religious aspects -- Islam

I. Title. II. Series: Human Developmnet (Herndon, Va.), no. 2
HF5387.B425 1996
174/4 0882971 96-16857
CIP

The views and opinions expressed in this work are not necessarily those of the Institute.

Printed in the United States of America by International Graphics
10710 Tucker Street, Beltsville, MD 20705-2223 USA
Tel.: (301) 595-5999 Fax: (301) 595-5888 e-mail: igfx@aol.com

TABLE OF CONTENTS

بسم الله الرحمن الرحيم

In the name of Allah the Beneficent, the Merciful

Preface

This is the first edition of *Islamic Business Ethics*. This book is directed at Muslim businessmen or business employees who have to deal with ethical situations on a day-to-day basis. I have attempted to present key principles of management from an Islamic point of view. I pray to Allah that it serves the purpose for which it was written—that of helping Muslims engaged in business to act in accordance to the Islamic system of ethics.

I assume complete responsibility for all views expressed in the book. I apologize for any mistake that may have gone unnoticed. I would like to acknowledge the contributions of Dr. Iqbal Unus and Nadiah Beekun for their comments on the manuscript. Finally, I thank Drs. Ahmad Sakr and Gamal Badawi for their encouragement and guidance in multiple avenues, including writing this book.

Dr. Rafik I. Beekun
University of Nevada
November 1, 1996

ISLAMIC BUSINESS ETHICS

You are the best of peoples, evolved for mankind, enjoining what is right, forbidding what is wrong, and believing in Allah. (Qur'an 3:110)

Every day, individuals face ethical issues at work, and rarely know how to deal with them. A recent review of articles published in the *Wall Street Journal* during only one week in 1991 uncovered a whole array of issues being faced by employees: stealing, lying, fraud and deceit, etc.[1] Surveys both in the USA and internationally reveal rampant unethical behavior in businesses. For instance, a recent survey of 2,000 major US corporations revealed that the following ethical problems (arranged in order of importance) concerned managers: (1) drug and alcohol abuse, (2) employee theft, (3) conflicts of interest, (4) quality control issues, (5) discrimination in hiring and promotion, (6) misuse of proprietary information, (7) abuse of company expense accounts, (8) plant closings and lay-offs, (9) misuse of company assets, and (10) environmental pollution.[2] Internationally, the ethical values of businesses are also deficient. In a survey of 300 companies across the world, over 85% of senior executives indicated that the following issues were among their top ethical concerns: employee conflicts of interest, inappropriate gifts, sexual harassment, and unauthorized payments.[3]

Is it naive for a Muslim businessman to behave ethically in a globally, competitive environment? The answer is a resounding NO! In Islam, ethics governs all aspects of life. The conditions for everlasting success or *falāḥ* in Islam are the same for all Muslims–whether in conducting their business affairs or in carrying out their daily activities. Without specifying any situational context, Allah describes people who attain success as those who are "inviting to all that is good (*khayr*), enjoining what is right (*ma'rūf*) and

---

[1] Cherrington, J. O. and Cherrington, D. J. 1993. "A Menu of Moral Issues: One Week in the Life of the *Wall Street Journal*." *Journal of Business Ethics*, 11, pp. 255-265.

[2] *America's Most Pressing Ethical Problems*. 1990. Washington, DC: The Ethics Resource Center, p. 1.

[3] Baumann, Mary. 1987. "Ethics in Business." *USA Today*. She was citing data from the Conference Board.

forbidding what is wrong (*munkar*)."[4] Within a business context, however, what specific standards of conduct should a company follow? What is a Muslim businessman's responsibility to internal and external stakeholders? Although a firm's top executives may exhibit exemplary ethical behavior, how can middle- and lower-level managers be encouraged to behave in a similarly ethical manner? What are some guidelines that would ensure consistent ethical behavior in a Muslim business?

Defining Ethics

Ethics may be defined as the set of moral principles that distinguish what is right from what is wrong. It is a normative field because it prescribes what one should do or abstain from doing. Business ethics, sometimes referred to as management ethics or organizational ethics, simply limits its frame of reference to organizations.

Within an Islamic context, the term most closely related to ethics in the Qur'an is *khuluq*.[5] The Qur'an also uses a whole array of terms to describe the concept of goodness: *khayr* (goodness), *birr* (righteousness), *qisṭ* (equity), *'adl* (equilibrium and justice), *ḥaqq* (truth and right), *ma'rūf* (known and approved), and *taqwā* (piety). Pious actions are described as *ṣāliḥāt* and impious actions are described as *sayyi'āt*.[6]

Factors Influencing Ethical Behavior in Islam

What is considered ethical behavior may depend on the factors that define and affect ethical behavior. These factors have been identified in Figure 1.

Legal Interpretations

In secular societies, legal interpretations are based upon contemporary and often transient values and standards; in an Islamic society, these values and standards are guided by the Shari'ah and the collection of previous *fiqh* judgments. The result of these divergent approaches is amazing: at one time, it was legal and ethical in the United States to discriminate against women and minorities in hiring; now, affirmative action laws make it illegal to discriminate against these groups. By contrast, Islam has given women permanent and unalienable rights, and has never discriminated against minori-

---

[4] *Qur'an* 3:104.

[5] *Qur'an* 68:4. I thank Dr. Gamal Badawi for this suggestion.

[6] Fakhry, Majid. *Ethical Theories in Islam*. Leiden: E. J. Brill, 1991, pp. 12-13.

ties on any basis. For example, Abū Dharr reported that the Prophet (saaw) said to him,

> *You are not better than people with red or black skins unless you excel them in piety.*[7]

Figure 1
Determinants of Individual Ethics[8]

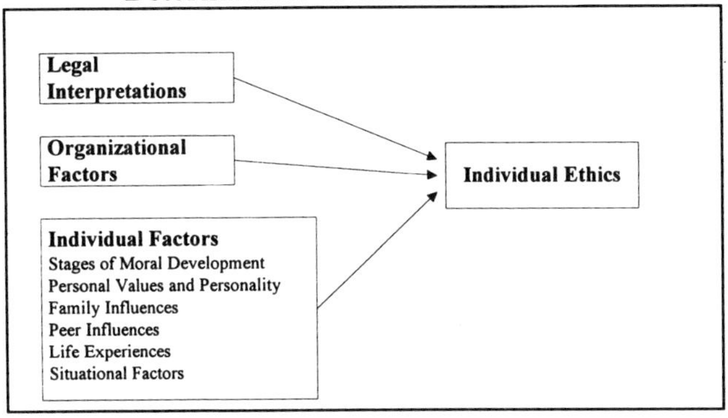

Similarly, the Islamic ethical system does not endorse the *caveat emptor* concept that many Western courts have considered valid in several shadowy cases. Thus, Anas ibn Mālik reports the following hadith:

> *Allah's Messenger (peace be upon him) forbade the sale of fruits till they are almost ripe. Anas was asked what is meant by "are almost ripe." He replied, "Till they become red." Allah's Messenger (peace be upon him) further said, "If Allah spoiled the fruits, what right would one have to take the money of one's brother (i.e., other people)?"*[9]

The Ḥanafis' interpretation of Islamic law reinforces this emphasis on equity and fairness:

> *If the vendor sells property as possessing a certain desirable quality and such property proves to be devoid of such quality,*

---

[7] Abū Dharr, *Mishkāt al Maṣābīḥ*, 5198 and transmitted by Aḥmad.

[8] Barney, Jay B. & Griffin, Ricky W. *The Management of Organizations*. © 1992 by Houghton Mifflin Company, p. 720. Adapted with permission.

[9] Anas ibn Mālik, *Ṣaḥīḥ al Bukhārī*, 3.403.

the purchaser has the option of either canceling the sale, or of accepting the thing sold for the whole of the fixed price. This is called option for misdescription.[10]

Organizational Factors

The organization too can affect influence participants' behavior. One of the key sources of organizational influence is the degree of commitment of the organization's leader to ethical conduct. This commitment can be communicated through a code of ethics, policy statements, speeches, publications, etc. For example, Xerox Corporation has a 15 page ethical code, one section of which states:

We're honest with our customers. No deals, no bribes, no secrets, no fooling around with prices. A kickback in any form kicks anybody out. Anybody.

The above statement is clear and relates specific unethical behavior to negative consequences.

Codes of ethics are gaining in popularity in many organizations, and often vary from one industry to another. Although such codes may enhance ethical behavior among organizational participants, their use is sometimes inappropriate. Some organizations may be trading in or selling in *khamr* or other haram products or services; hence, the conduct of the whole organization is unethical. Developing and enforcing a code of ethics in this type of organization is clearly erroneous since Allah Ṣubḥānahu wa ta'ālā has said in the Qur'an:

They ask you concerning wine and gambling. Say, "In them is great sin, and some profit for men; but the sin is greater than the profit."[11]

In general, however, organizations engaged in *ḥalāl* businesses can foster ethical behavior through the development of an Islamic code of ethics.

---

[10] *Al Majallah* (The Ottoman Courts Manual [Ḥanafi]), Section II. Option for Misdescription, 310.

[11] *Qur'an* 2:219.

Individual Factors

Individuals come to work with different values. Factors affecting one's ethical behavior include: stages of moral development, personal values and morals, family influences, peer influences, and life experiences.

Stages of Moral Development. The Prophet (saaw) suggested that individuals undergo two stages of moral development: the minor or pre-pubescent stage and the adulthood stage. In a hadith narrated by 'Ā'ishah (rah), she narrated that:

> *The Apostle of Allah (peace be upon him) said: 'There are three (persons) whose actions are not recorded: a sleeper till he awakes, an idiot till he is restored to reason, and a boy till he reaches puberty.'*[12]

From the above hadith, two facts can be inferred. First, certain types of people are not responsible for their behavior: the sleeper, the lunatic and the child before puberty. Second, an individual is not responsible for his actions until the age of reason.

In addition to physical and mental development, Islamic scholars[13] have suggested that there are three states or stages of the development of the human soul or *nafs*: (1) *ammārah* (12:53), which is prone to evil, and, if not checked and controlled, will lead to perdition; (2) *lawwāmah*, (75:2), which feels consciousness of evil, and resists it, asks for Allah's grace and pardon after repentance and tries to amend; it hopes to reach salvation; (3) *muṭma'innah* (89:27), the highest stage of all, when the soul achieves full rest and satisfaction after *'aql* (intellect) has checked the evil tendencies of man.[14] If a Muslim persists in behaving unethically, he is succumbing to the *ammārah*; if he is behaving Islamically, he is fighting the evil impulses of the *ammārah*, and responding to the directions of the *lawwāmah* and the *muṭma'innah*. Of course, what will govern his ethical behavior and the interaction among these three states of the soul is his level of *taqwā* or piety. Depending on which level his *nafs* is at and whether he is winning or losing the battle against temptation and evil, he may be more or less prone towards behaving ethically.

---

[12] 'Ā'ishah, Umm al Mu'minīn, Abū Dāwūd, 4384.

[13] Rizvi, S. A. *Muslim Tradition in Psychotherapy and Modern Trends*. Lahore, Pakistan: Institute of Islamic Culture.

[14] Ibid., pp. 50-51.

Personal Values and Personality. An individual's values and morals will also influence his or her ethical standards. A person who stresses honesty will behave very differently from another who does not respect other people's property. Interestingly, in Islam, the decay and eventual disappearance of honesty is a sign of the imminence of the Day of Judgment. Abū Hurayrah reports:

> *While the Prophet (peace be upon him) was saying something in a gathering, a Bedouin came and asked him, "When would the Hour (Doomsday) take place?" Allah's Apostle (peace be upon him) continued his talk, so some people said that Allah's Apostle (peace be upon him) had heard the question, but did not like what that Bedouin had asked. Some of them said that Allah's Apostle (peace be upon him) had not heard it.*
>
> *When the Prophet (peace be upon him) finished his speech, he said, "Where is the questioner, who inquired about the Hour (Doomsday)?" The Bedouin said, "I am here, O Allah's Apostle (peace be upon him)." Then the Prophet (peace be upon him) said, "When honesty is lost, then wait for the Hour (Doomsday)." The Bedouin said, "How will that be lost?" The Prophet (peace be upon him) said, "When the power or authority comes in the hands of unfit persons, then wait for the Hour (Doomsday)."*[15]

A key personality variable which may affect the ethical behavior of an individual is his/her locus of control. The locus of control of an individual affects the degree to which he perceives his behavior as influencing his life. An individual has an internal locus of control if he/she believes that he/she can control the events in his/her life. As a result, internals are likely to take responsibility for the outcomes of their behavior. Conversely, an individual with an external locus of control believes that fate or luck or other people affect his life. Such an individual is likely to believe that external forces cause him to behave either ethically or unethically. Overall, internals are more likely than externals to make ethical decisions, are less willing to cave

---

[15] *Ṣaḥīḥ al Bukhārī*, 1.56

in to pressure to behave unethically, and will resist hurting others, even when ordered to do so by a superior.[16]

Family Influences. Individuals start to form ethical standards as children. The Prophet (saaw) emphasized the importance of family nurturing when he said:

> *Command your children to pray when they become seven years old, and discipline them for it (prayer) when they become ten years old; and arrange their beds (to sleep) separately.*[17]

Here, the implication is that if you wish your children to grow up as good Muslims, you need to start shaping them from a young age. Children are likely to develop high ethical standards if they perceive other family members as consistently adhering to high standards, and if they are rewarded for ethical behavior but punished for being untruthful, stealing etc. Mixed messages from parents are likely to result in unethical behavior on the part of the child. An example of mixed messages is that of a child who is told that stealing is bad; at the same time, he is given supplies "borrowed" from the parents' office at work.

Peer Influences. As children grow and are admitted to school, they are influenced by the peers with whom they interact daily. Thus, if a child's friends engage in drawing graffiti, the child may imitate them. If the child's peers avoid such behavior, the child is likely to behave accordingly.

Life Experiences. Whether positive or negative, key events affect the lives of individuals and determine their ethical beliefs and behavior. Malcolm X's Hajj experience had a major impact on his later years as a Muslim:

> *There were tens of thousands of pilgrims, from all over the world. They were of all colors, from blue-eyed blonds to black-*

---

[16] Lefcourt, H. M. *Locus of Control: Current Trends in Theory and Research.* Hillsdale, NJ: Erlbaum, 1982, 2d edition.

[17] 'Abd Allāh ibn Amr ibn al 'Āṣ, Abū Dāwūd, 0495. In discussing this hadith with Dr. Gamal Badawi, he indicated that Islam is not for harsh "spanking" of children. They should, of themselves, wish to follow the role models presented by their parents and want to observe the regular prayers by age ten. If they do not, then light but appropriate discipline should be administered.

skinned Africans. But we were all participating in the same ritual, displaying a spirit of unity and brotherhood that my experience in America had led me to believe never could exist between the white and the non-white.

America needs to understand Islam, because this is the one religion that erases from its society the race problem. [...] I have never before seen sincere *and* true *brotherhood practiced by all colors together, irrespective of their color.*

You may be shocked by these words coming from me. But on this pilgrimage, what I have seen, and experienced, has forced me to re-arrange *much of thought-patterns previously held, and to* toss aside *some of my previous conclusions.*[18]

Situational Factors. People may behave unethically in certain situations because they may see no way out. For example, a manager may record fictitious sales in order to cover losses within his area of responsibility. According to Islam, debt is a major reason why individuals behave unethically. In a hadith narrated by 'Ā'ishah (raw),

Somebody said to [the Prophet], "Why do you so frequently seek refuge with Allah from being in debt?" The Prophet (peace be upon him) replied, "A person in debt tells lies whenever he speaks, and breaks promises whenever he makes (them)."[19]

Since indebtedness is likely to lead to unethical conduct, Muslim lenders are encouraged to show leniency to debtors. At the same time, debtors are urged to repay debts promptly.

The Islamic Ethical System

The Islamic ethical system differs from secular ethical systems and from the moral code advocated by other religions. Throughout civilization, these secular models[20] assumed moral codes that were transient and myopic since

---

[18] Haley, Alex. 1965. *The Autobiography of Malcolm X*. New York: Ballantine Books, p. 340.
[19] 'Ā'ishah, *Ṣaḥīḥ al Bukhārī*, 1.795.
[20] Badawi, Jamal. *Islamic Teachings*. Halifax, NS Canada. Package II, series F, cassettes 1 and 2.

they were based on the values of their human founders, e.g., epicurianism or happiness for happiness's sake. These models generally proposed a system of ethics divorced from religion. At the same time, the moral code adopted by other religions have often stressed values that de-emphasize our existence in this world. For example, Christianity by its overemphasis on monasticism encourages its adherents to retire from the hustle and bustle of daily life. By contrast, the moral code embedded in Islamic ethics emphasizes the relation of man to His Creator. Because God is Perfect and Omniscient, Muslims have a code that is neither timebound nor biased by human whims.[21] The Islamic code of ethics is enforceable at all times because Its Creator and Monitor is closer to man than his jugular vein, and has perfect, eternal knowledge. To spell out Islam's moral code, we will now compare alternate ethics systems to the Islamic ethical system.

Alternate Ethics Systems

Contemporary ethics differs from the Islamic ethical system in multiple ways. Six ethical systems now dominate ethical thinking in general. These are summarized in Table 1.

Relativism

Relativism stresses that no single, universal criterion can be used to determine whether an action is ethical or not. Each person uses his or her own criterion, and this criterion may vary from culture to culture. As a result, the ethical character of different social values and behaviors are seen within specific cultural contexts.[22] Hence, businessmen engaging in activities in another country are bound by its norms and values.

Several problems are associated with this ethical system. First, the relativism school is self-centered; it focuses solely on the individual and excludes any interaction with or input from the outside.[23] This approach is in direct contradiction to Islam. Islam stresses that an individual's ethical behavior and values should be based on criteria enunciated in the Qur'an and the Sunnah. Second, relativism implies an inherent laziness in the decision-maker; he or she may justify his or her behavior by simply referring to criteria based on self-interest. Islam, by contrast, stays away from decisions based only on one's perception of a situation. The principle of consul-

---

[21] Loc. cit.
[22] Weiss, p. 64.
[23] Loc. cit.

tation or *shūrā* with others is an intrinsic part of the Muslim businessman's decision-making apparatus. Egoism has no place in Islam.

Table 1 Overview of Six Major Ethical Systems[24]	
Alternate Ethical Systems	Decision-Making Criteria
Relativism (Self-interest)	Ethical decisions are made on the basis of self-interest and needs.
Utilitarianism (Calculation of costs and benefits)	Ethical decisions are made on the basis of the outcome(s) resulting from these decisions. An action is ethical if it results in the greatest benefit for the largest number of people.
Universalism (Duty)	Ethical decisions stress the intention of the decision or action. Similar decisions should be reached by everyone under similar circumstances.
Rights (Individual entitlement)	Ethical decisions stress a single value, liberty, and are based on individual rights ensuring freedom of choice.
Distributive Justice (Fairness and equity)	Ethical decisions stress a single value, justice, and ensure an equitable distribution of wealth and benefits.
Eternal Law (Scripture)	Ethical decisions are made on the basis of eternal law which is revealed in scripture.

Utilitarianism

From Cicero to Jeremy Bentham and J. S. Mill, the utilitarian approach to ethics has survived almost two millennia. It holds that "the moral worth of personal conduct can be determined solely by the consequences of that behavior."[25] An action is ethical if it results in the greatest benefit or "good" for the largest number of people. Hence, utilitarianism[26] is very outcome-oriented.

Problems associated with this ethical system are many. First, who determines what "good" is for the maximum number of people? Is it wealth, pleasure, or health? Second, what happens to the minority? If the majority in the US should decide that the doctrine of free love will rule the land, who will

---

[24] Adapted with permission from Weiss, J. W. *Business Ethics: A Managerial, Stakeholder Approach.* Belmont, CA: Wadsworth Publishing, © 1994. Reproduced with permission from the publisher.

[25] Hosmer, p. 109.

[26] I am discussing *act utilitarianism* instead of *rule utilitarianism.*

protect the interests of the minority who believes in matrimony and monogamous relationships as prescribed by God? Third, how are costs and benefits to be assessed when nonquantifiable issues such as health are to be dealt with? Fourth, individual rights and responsibilities are ignored in favor of the collective rights and responsibilities.[27] This is contrary to Islam because both it considers both individual and collective rights to be important. Further, a Muslim cannot blame the ummah for his actions; each person is ultimately responsible for his or her actions as an individual.

> *One day every soul will come up struggling for itself and every soul will be recompensed (fully) for all its actions and none will be unjustly dealt with.*[28]

Finally, utilitarianism determines the ethical nature of future actions through weighing their costs against their benefits, and can easily be carried to an extreme. This danger can be easily seen in the microeconomics approach to business ethics that dominates much of Western business's bottom-line thinking.

Microeconomics emphasizes the rule of *pareto optimality*. This rule stresses the efficient utilization of resources to satisfy consumer wants, rules out any need to consider ethical issues, and overemphasizes profit maximization. Milton Friedman summarizes the microeconomic approach to managerial ethics as follows:

> *Few trends could so thoroughly undermine the very foundations of our free society as the acceptance by corporate officials of a social responsibility other than to make as much money for their stockholders as possible.*[29]

Contrary to the microeconomic approach to business ethics, profit maximization is not the ultimate goal or only ethical outcome of trade in Islam. Allah Ṣubḥānahu wa taʻālā has said in the Qur'an:

---

[27] Weiss, 67.

[28] *Qur'an* 16:111.

[29] Friedman, Milton. 1962. *Capitalism and Freedom*. Chicago: University of Chicago Press, p. 133.

Wealth and sons are allurements of the life of this world; But the things that endure, good deeds, are the best in the sight of your Lord, as rewards, and best as the foundation for hopes.[30]

Universalism

In contrast to utilitarianism's emphasis on the outcomes of decisions, universalism focuses on the intention of the decision or action. The key principle underlying the universalism school is Kant's principle of the **categorical imperative**. This principle is in two parts. First, a person should choose to act only if he/she is willing to let everyone on earth in a similar circumstance make the exact same decision and act the exact same way.[31] Second, others should be treated as ends, worthy of dignity and respect, not just as means towards an end. Consequently, this approach focuses on the *duty* that an individual owes towards other individuals and humanity.

Problems with universalism relate to what Kant means by *duty*.[32] According to him, only when we act from duty is our action ethical. If we acted simply out of feeling or self-interest, then our action has no moral worth. Islam, too, looks at the intention of the person committing an act.

'Alqamah ibn Waqqās al Laythī said, "I heard 'Umar, while he was on the minbar (pulpit) delivering a sermon, saying, 'I heard the Messenger of Allah say, "O people! Behold, the action(s) are but (judged) by intention(s) and every man shall have but that which he intended."'

Thus he whose migration was for Allah and His Messenger, his migration was for Allah and His Messenger, and he whose migration was to achieve some worldly benefit or to take some woman in marriage, his migration was for that for which he migrated."[33]

However, good intentions alone do not make an unethical act ethical. As pointed out by Yūsuf al Qaraḍāwī, "good intentions do not make the *ḥarām* acceptable."[34] Whenever a Muslim follows up a good intention with a per-

---

[30] *Qur'an* 18:46.
[31] Weiss, 68.
[32] William H. Shaw. *Business Ethics*. Belmont, CA: Wadsworth, 1991, p. 57.
[33] 'Umar ibn al Khaṭṭāb, *Ṣaḥīḥ al Bukhārī*, hadith no. 1.1.
[34] Al Qaraḍāwī, Yūsuf. *Al Ḥalāl wa al Ḥarām fi al Islām*. Indianapolis, USA: American Trust Publications, p. 11.

missible action, his action becomes an act of worship. Indeed, the Prophet (saaw) said:

> *In the morning alms are due from every bone in man's fingers and toes. Salutation to everyone he meets is alms; enjoining good is alms; forbidding what is disreputable is alms; removing what is harmful from the road is alms; having sexual intercourse with his wife is alms. The people asked, "He fulfills his desire, Apostle of Allah; is it alms?" He replied, "Tell me, if he fulfilled his desire where he had no right, would he commit a sin?" [...].*[35]

Moreover, if an act is *ḥarām*, then Islam does not allow this *ḥarām* act to be used as a means to achieve a good end. In other words, the end does not justify the means. As the Prophet (saaw) explained, if someone acquires wealth through *ḥarām* means and then gives charity from it, he will not benefit from it and the burden of sin still remains.[36]

Rights

The rights approach to ethics stresses a single value: liberty. To be considered ethical, decisions and actions must be based on individual rights ensuring freedom of choice. This approach suggests that individual have moral rights that are non-negotiable. For example, every American is legally guaranteed the rights to freedom, dignity and choice. These rights, in turn, lead to mutual obligations among stakeholders. Thus, the employee has a right to a fair wage and to a safe working environment. The employer has a right to expect his trade secrets not be divulged by his employees.

The rights approach to ethics can be abused. Some individuals may insist that their rights take priority over the rights of others, and inequity may result. Rights also may need to have limits. Industry regulations that benefit society may still trample on the rights of certain individuals or groups. For example, overzealous industry regulations that require a certain type of dress code for safety reasons may unnecessarily set aside Muslim women's desire for modest clothing.

---

[35] Abū Dharr, in Abū Dāwūd, hadith no. 5223.

[36] Al Qaraḍāwī, p. 32. Please note that necessity does dictate exceptions, and Islam is not oblivious to the crises and emergencies that one may face. As seen in *Qur'an* 2:173, Allah will allow a Muslim to eat the *ḥarām* (e.g., pork, blood, dead animals) if he is faced with certain starvation. Under such duress, a Muslim need not embrace the *ḥarām* eagerly and should return to the *ḥalāl* as soon as possible. See al Qaraḍāwī, pp. 36-38.

Contrary to the myths perpetuated by orientalists, Islam is for freedom. For example, it allows humankind the freedom to choose his own faith. Allah says in the Qur'an:

> *Let there be no compulsion in religion: Truth stands out clear from error: whoever rejects evil and believes in Allah has grasped the most trustworthy handhold, that never breaks. And Allah hears and knows all things.*[37]

Islam, however, is for balance and rejects the notion of liberty without accountability. Man bears responsibility for his actions. Counterintuitively, the greatest freedom is attained by submission. Indeed, once a person believes in Allah, he attains a different kind of freedom:[38]

> *Say: He is Allah, the One and Only. Allah, the Eternal, Absolute: He begets not nor is He begotten. And there is none like unto Him.*[39]

Islam frees the Muslim from servitude to anyone or anything except Allah.

Distributive Justice

This approach to ethics revolves around a single value: justice. To be considered ethical, decisions and actions should ensure an equitable distribution of wealth and benefits and burdens. There are five principles that may be used to ensure this proper distribution of benefits and burdens:[40]

1. *To each an equal share*. When a company distributes its yearly bonuses, each eligible party should receive a portion equal to every other eligible party.
2. *To each according to individual need.* Resources should be allocated to individuals or departments in terms of the level of need they experience.
3. *To each according to individual effort.* Everything else being equal, employees should receive pay increases or paycuts in direct proportion to their level of effort.

---

[37] *Qur'an* 2:256.

[38] Sayed Kotb. *Social Justice in Islam*. New York: Octagon Books, 1980, p. 32.

[39] *Qur'an* 112:1-4.

[40] Shaw, pp. 86-87.

4. *To each according to social contribution.* If a company is making a special effort to address social issues, e.g., environmental pollution, it should receive rewards that other companies less careful about the environment may not get.
5. *To each according to merit.* Promotion, hiring and firing decisions should be done on the basis of individual merit and no other consideration, e.g., nepotism, favoritism or personal bias.

Islam is in favor of justice. According to the Qur'an, the role of the message delivered by His prophets has been to establish justice.[41] Muslims in position of leadership are encouraged to deal justly with their followers or subordinates.

> *The Prophet of Allah (peace be upon him) said, "A commander (of the Muslims) is a shield for them. They fight behind him and they are protected by (him from tyrants and aggressors). If he enjoins fear of God, the Exalted and Glorious, and dispenses justice, there will be a (great) reward for him; and if he enjoins otherwise, it redounds on him."*[42]

The Islamic principles of distributive justice include the following:[43]

- Every person is entitled to own property individually or in partnership with others. State ownership of critical resources is allowed if it is in the public interest.[44]
- The poor have a claim on part of the wealth accumulated by the rich to the extent that the basic needs of everyone in society are met. Since Allah has honored the descendants of Adam and provided good things[45] for them, the basic needs of all humankind must be met. This is why the blessings of *infāq*, voluntary spending to take care of the poor, are emphasized in the Qur'an as well as in several hadiths. For example, the Prophet (saw) said:

---

41 *Qur'an* 57:25.

42 Abū Hurayrah, in *Ṣaḥīḥ Muslim*, hadith no. 4542.

43 Ahmad, Ziauddin. 1991. *Islam, Poverty and Income Distribution.* Leicester, UK: The Islamic Foundation, pp. 15-16.

44 See Ahmad, 1991 for more details.

45 *Qur'an* 17:70.

The most excellent ṣadaqah *consists in your satisfying a hungry stomach.*[46]

Islam, however, does not aim to remove all differences in income and wealth. The existence of these differences form part of Allah's plan. They serve towards the smooth functioning of the economy.[47]

- Human exploitation at any level, in any shape and under any circumstances is anti-Islamic and must be ended. For example, the sweatshops that exploit the poor in exchange for paltry wages in order to keep production costs down are un-Islamic.

In general, Islam agrees with all of the principles of the distributive justice approach to ethics, but in a balanced manner. Islam does not endorse blind justice. Need alone may not require justice. Thus, a Muslim who has tried to get out of an oppressive situation is more deserving of help than another person who is simply claiming his share from the wealth of the rich.

> *When angels take the souls of those who die in sin against their souls, they say, "In what (plight) were you? They reply, "Weak and oppressed were we in the earth." They*[48] *say, "Was not the earth of Allah spacious enough for you to move yourselves away (from evil)?" Such men will find their abode in Hell. What an evil refuge!*[49]

Again, merit or social contribution alone do not require special consideration since these are often viewed as correlates of rank. Islamic justice can neither be modified nor suppressed by invoking rank and/or privilege. For example,

> *A lady committed theft during the lifetime of Allah's Apostle in the ghazwah of al Fatḥ, (i.e., conquest of Makkah). Her folk went to Usāmah ibn Zayd to intercede for her (with the Prophet). When Usāmah interceded for her with Allah's Apostle, the color of the face of Allah's Apostle changed and he said, "Do you intercede with me in a matter involving one of the legal punishments prescribed by Allah?" Usāmah said, "O*

---

46 Anas Ibn Mālik, in *Mishkāt al Maṣābīḥ*, 1946.
47 See *Qur'an* 43:32, and Ahmad, 1991, pp. 19-20.
48 The angels.
49 *Qur'an* 4:99.

Allah's Apostle! Ask Allah's forgiveness for me." So in the afternoon, Allah's Apostle got up and addressed the people. He praised Allah as He deserved and then said, "Amma ba'du ! The nations prior to you were destroyed because if a noble amongst them stole, they used to excuse him, and if a poor person amongst them stole, they would apply (Allah's) legal punishment to him. By Him in whose hand Muhammad's soul is, if Fāṭimah, the daughter of Muhammad stole, I would cut her hand." Then Allah's Apostle gave his order in the case of that woman and her hand was cut off. Afterwards her repentance proved sincere and she got married. 'Ā'ishah said, "That lady used to visit me and I used to convey her demands to Allah's Apostle."[50]

Compare the above decision of Muhammad (saaw) to the inconsistent treatment of law breakers in the contemporary Muslim world and the United States. The recent trial and acquittal of O J. Simpson illustrates what happens when ethics is derailed. Another example of inconsistency in the law is the treatment accorded to cocaine and crack addicts. Both types of drugs are equally *ḥarām* and harmful. Nevertheless, since cocaine is the Caucasian American drug of choice, the punishment for cocaine users is less severe than what is dealt to users of crack. Crack is cocaine in its raw form, but is primarily used by African Americans.

Eternal Law

Ethical decisions are made on the basis of eternal law which is revealed in scripture and in the state of nature. Many writers (including Thomas Aquinas) believe that by studying <u>either</u> the scripture or nature, man will become ethically aware.

Islam takes a different perspective. Basing himself on the Qur'an, namely verses 96:1-5; 68:1-2; and 55:1-3, Ṭāhā Jābir al 'Alwānī concludes that humankind has been enjoined by Allah to perform two different kinds of readings <u>simultaneously</u>: a reading of Allah's revelation (the Qur'an) and a reading of the natural universe. Those who undertake only the first type of reading become ascetics. Sometimes, such a reading makes them become imbalanced and incapable of independent thinking. They give up all independent actions and fail in their responsibilities as the stewards of Allah

[50] *Ṣaḥīḥ al Bukhārī*, hadith 5.597.

(*istikhlāf*) or the keepers of His trust (*amānah*).[51] Those who stress only the second reading "are powerless to answer the 'ultimate' questions," and generally dismiss everything beyond their abilities to perceive by means of the senses as 'supernatural.'"[52] Worse, should they believe at all, they believe in a god that they have themselves fashioned, often equating that god with nature itself. Such a one-sided reading can only lead to *shirk* or nonsensical theories such as existentialism, pantheism or even dialectical materialism. Hence, Muslims should perform both readings simultaneously:

> *The Qur'an is a guide to the real–existential, and the real–existential is a guide to the Qur'an. [true] knowledge may not be attained except by means of a complementary reading of these two sources.*[53]

As a result of these two readings, the Islamic code of ethics is unlike the moral code advocated by other religions. Christianity as well as some eastern religions emphasize the transience of this life, and value meditation and retirement from this world. Islam, on the other hand, stresses that piety is not achieved by relinquishing the life of this world. It is through the active participation in the day-to-day affairs of this world and through the struggle in this life against evil that a Muslim proves himself. The idea of the active participation of man in the material world is part of the concept of *tazkīyah*, namely growth and purification, and is important with respect to Islamic economic theory.[54] In other words, a Muslim is expected to participate in *dunyā* with the proviso that any material enhancement and growth must lead to social justice and spiritual upliftment of both the *ummah* and himself. Allah emphasizes that ultimate goal with the story of Qārūn:

> *The reward of Allah (In the Hereafter) is best for those who believe and work righteousness: but this none shall attain, save those who steadfastly persevere (in good).*[55]

---

[51] Ṭāhā Jābir al 'Alwānī. 1995. *The Islamization of Knowledge: Yesterday and Today*. Translation into English by Yusuf Talal DeLorenzo. Herndon, Virginia: International Institute of Islamic Thought, pp. 6-13.
[52] Loc. cit., p. 8.
[53] Loc. cit. p. 11.
[54] T. Gambling and R. Karim. *Business and Accounting Ethics in Islam*. London: Mansell, 1991, p. 33.
[55] *Qur'an* 28:80.

While participating in this life, a Muslim must remember to be consistent both in his acts of worship and in his day-to-day life. Observing the five pillars of Islam is not enough for a Muslim; he also needs to conform to the Islamic code of ethics.

> *Allah's Apostle (peace be upon him) said, "Do you know who is poor?" They (the Companions of the Prophet) said, "A poor man amongst us is one who has neither dirham with him nor wealth." He (the Prophet) said, "The poor of my ummah would be he who would come on the Day of Resurrection with prayers and fasts and zakat but (he would find himself bankrupt on that day as he would have exhausted his funds of virtues) since he hurled abuses upon others, brought calumny against others and unlawfully consumed the wealth of others and shed the blood of others and beat others, and his virtues would be credited to the account of one (who suffered at his hand). And if his good deeds fall short to clear the account, then his sins would be entered in (his account) and he would be thrown in the Hell-Fire."*[56]

The eternal law in Islam is not limited to matters of religion; it permeates all aspects of a Muslim's life.

Islamic Ethical System

Based upon the above discussion, some of the key parameters of the Islamic ethical system have been uncovered, and can be summarized as follows:

- Actions and decisions are judged to be ethical depending on the intention of the individual. Allah is Omniscient, and knows our intention completely and perfectly.
- Good intentions followed by good actions are considered as acts of worship. *Ḥalāl* intentions cannot make *ḥarām* actions *ḥalāl.*
- Islam allows an individual the freedom to believe and act however he/she desires, but not at the expense of accountability and justice.
- Belief in Allah endows the individual with complete freedom from anything or anybody except Allah.

---

[56] Abū Hurayrah, *Ṣaḥīḥ Muslim*, hadith no. 6251.

- Decisions that benefit the majority or a minority are not necessarily ethical in themselves. Ethics is not a numbers game.
- Islam uses an open system approach to ethics, not a closed, self-oriented system. Egoism has no place in Islam.
- Ethical decisions are based on a simultaneous reading of the Qur'an and the natural universe.
- Unlike the ethical systems advocated by many other religions, Islam encourages humankind to experience *tazkīyah* through active participation in this life. By behaving ethically in the midst of the tests of this *dunyā*, Muslims prove their worth to Allah.

In contrast to all the approaches summarized in Table 1, the Islamic ethical system is neither fragmented nor unidimensional. It is part of the Islamic view of life and therefore complete. There is internal consistency, or '*adl*, or equilibrium, within an individual's code of conduct. This axiom of equilibrium is at the heart of the following Qur'anic *āyāt*:

> *Thus have We made of you an ummah justly balanced that you might be witnesses over the nations and the Apostle a witness over yourselves;*[57]

To further develop the Islamic ethical system, we need to investigate what axioms guide the ethical philosophy of Islam. These have been implicitly referred to so far, but are discussed in detail in the next section.

Axioms of Islamic Ethical Philosophy

Five key axioms[58] govern Islamic ethics: unity, equilibrium, free will, responsibility, and benevolence, and are summarized in Table 2.

Unity

Unity, as reflected in the concept of *tawḥīd*, is the vertical dimension of Islam. It combines into a homogeneous whole all the different aspects of a Muslim's life: economic, political, religious, and social, and stresses the idea

---

[57] *Qur'an* 2:143.

[58] Naqvi, S. (1981), p. 48-57 introduces the first four axioms, but the ethical work of al Ghazālī suggests that the concept of *'adl* includes not only equilibrium but also justice and equity, and that there may be an additional axiomatic principle, that of *iḥsān* or benevolence.

of consistency and order throughout. The axiom of unity has lasting effects on the Muslim:[59]

1. Since a Muslim looks upon everything in the world as belonging to Allah, the same Lord to Whom he himself belongs, he cannot be biased in his thinking and behavior. His vision is wider, and his sense of service is not restricted to any specific sphere or group. Any thought of racism or caste system is inconsistent with his thinking.

Table 2
Axioms of Islamic Ethical Philosophy[60]

Axiom	Definition
Unity	Related to the concept of *tawḥīd*. The political, economic, social, and religious aspects of man's life form a homogeneous whole, which is consistent from within, as well as integrated with the vast universe without. This is the vertical dimension of Islam.
Equilibrium	Related to the concept of *'adl*. A sense of balance among the various aspects of a man's life mentioned above in order to produce the best social order. This sense of balance is achieved through conscious purpose. This is the horizontal dimension of Islam.
Free will	Man's ability to act without external coercion within the parameters of Allah's creation and as Allah's trustee on earth.
Responsibility	Man's need to be accountable for his actions.
Benevolence	*Iḥsān* or an action that benefits persons other than those from whom the action proceeds without any obligation.

2. Since Only Allah is all powerful and omniscient, the Muslim is indifferent to, independent of, and fearless of, all powers other than

[59] Maudoodi, Sayyid Abul A'lā. 1977. *Towards Understanding Islam*. Tacoma Park, MD: International Graphics Printing Service, pp. 74-78.
[60] Naqvi, S. (1981), pp. 48-57.

Him. He is not overawed by anybody's greatness, and will not allow himself to be coerced into performing unethical acts by anybody. Since Allah Ṣubḥānahu wa ta'ālā can take away just as He can give, the Muslim will be humble and modest.

3. Since he is convinced that only Allah Ṣubḥānahu wa ta'ālā can help him, he never despairs of Allah's Help and Mercy. No man or animal has the power to deprive him of his life before his appointed time; Allah only has the power to take away his life. He will act bravely in doing what is ethical and Islamic.

4. The most important effect of *lā ilāha illa Allāh* is that the Muslim will obey and observe Allah's law. He believes that Allah knows everything open or hidden, and that he cannot hide anything, intention or act from his Lord. Consequently, he will avoid what is forbidden, and engage in what is good.

Application of the Unity Axiom to Business Ethics: Based on the above discussion of the unity axiom, a Muslim businessman will not:

- Discriminate among his employees, suppliers, buyers, or any other stake-holder on the basis of race, color, sex, or religion. This is consistent with Allah's purpose for creating mankind:

  O mankind! Lo! We have created you male and female, and have made you nations and tribes, that you may know one another.[61]

- Be coerced into unethical practices, since he has only Allah to fear and love. He follows the same, unified code of behavior whether he is in the mosque, earning a living or acting out other aspects of his life. He will be content.

  "Say: Lo! My worship and my sacrifice and my living and my dying are all for Allah, Lord of the Worlds."[62]

---

[61] *Qur'an* 49:13.
[62] *Qur'an* 6:163.

- Hoard his wealth avariciously. The concept of *amānah* or trust is of critical importance to him because he knows that any worldly merit is transient, and must be used wisely. A Muslim is not solely guided by profits, and is not seeking to accumulate wealth at any cost. He realizes that:
-

> *Wealth and sons are allurements of the life of this world; but things that endure—good deeds—are best in the sight of your Lord, as rewards, and best as (the foundation for) hopes.*[63]

Equilibrium

Equilibrium, or *'adl*, describes the horizontal dimension of Islam, and relates to the all-embracing harmony in the universe.[64] The law and order that we see in the universe reflect this delicate balance. As Allah says,

> *Lo! We have created every thing by measure.*[65]

The property of equilibrium is more than a characteristic of nature; it is a dynamic characteristic which each Muslim must strive for in his or her life. The need for balance and equilibrium is stressed by Allah when He labels the Muslim ummah as *ummatun wasaṭun*. To maintain a sense of balance between those who have and those who have not, Allah stresses the importance of giving and condemns the practice of conspicuous consumption:

> *And spend of your substance in the cause of Allah. And make not your own hands contribute to (your) destruction; But do good; for Allah loves those who do good.*[66]

Simultaneously, Allah is not urging extreme asceticism. Balance and moderation are key; He describes those "who will be rewarded with the highest place in heaven" as:

> *Those who, when they spend, are not extravagant and not niggardly, but hold a just (balance) between those two extremes;*

---

[63] *Qur'an* 18:46.

[64] See Maudoodi, *Towards Understanding Islam*, pp. 2-3 for an in-depth discussion of equilibrium.

[65] *Qur'an* 54:59.

[66] *Qur'an* 2:195.

Those who invoke not with Allah, any other god, [...]; those who witness no falsehood and, if they pass by futility, they pass by it with honorable (avoidance); those who, when they are admonished with the signs of their Lord, droop not down at them as if they were deaf or blind: [...][67]

Application of the Equilibrium Axiom to Business Ethics. The principle of equilibrium or balance applies both figuratively and literally to business. For example, Allah admonishes Muslim businessmen to:

Give full measure when you measure and weigh with a balance that is straight: that is the most fitting and the most advantageous in the final determination.[68]

It is interesting that another meaning of *'adl* is justice and equity.[69] As can be seen in the above *āyāt*, a balanced transaction is also equitable and just.[70] The Qur'an uses the term *'adl* in this sense. Overall, Islam does not aim to create a society of martyr-like merchants, doing business for purely philanthropic reason. Instead, Islam wants to curb man's propensity for covetousness and his love for possessions. As a result, miserliness[71] and a spendthrift mode of conduct have both been condemned in the Qur'an and in the Hadith.

Free Will

To a certain degree, man has been granted the free will to steer his own life as Allah's vicegerent on earth.[72] Notwithstanding the fact that he is completely regulated by the law governing Allah's creation, he has been endowed with the ability to think and form judgments, to adopt whatever course of life he wishes and, most importantly, to act in accordance with

---

67 *Qur'an* 25:67-68, 72-73.

68 *Qur'an* 17:35.

69 Umar-ud-din, Muhammad. *The Ethical Philosophy of al Ghazzālī*. Lahore, Pakistan: Sh. Muhammad Ashraf, 1991, p. 241.

70 The notion of balance being consistent with the concepts of equity and justice is part of equity theory in management; see Gibson, J. L., Ivancevich, J. M. and Donnelly, J. H. (1994). *Organizations: Behavior, Structure and Processes*. Burr Ridge, IL: Irwin.

71 "Those who hoard up gold and silver and spend them not in the way of Allah...." *Qur'an* 9:34.

72 *Qur'an* 2:30.

whatever code of conduct he chooses. Unlike other creatures in Allah's universe, he can choose how ethically or unethically he will behave.

> *Say, "The Truth is from your Lord. Let him who will, believe, and let him who will, reject (it)."* [73]

Once he chooses to become a Muslim, he must submit his will to Allah's. He joins the collective of the ummah, and assumes his rightful position as Allah's trustee on earth. He agrees to behave according to the code that Allah has revealed for his individual and social life. Now "his entire life has become one of submission to God, and there is no conflict in his personality."[74] Free will co-exists with unity and equilibrium.

Application of the Free Will Axiom to Business Ethics. Based upon the axiom of free will, man has the freedom to make a contract and either honor or break it. A Muslim, who has submitted to the will of Allah, will honor all contracts.

> *O you who believe! Fulfill (all) obligations.*[75]

It is important to note that Allah is directing the above verse explicitly to Muslims. As Yūsuf 'Alī suggests, the word *'uqūd* is a multidimensional construct. It implies (a) the divine obligations that spring from our spiritual nature and our relation to Allah, (b) our social obligations such as a marriage contract, (c) our political obligations such as a treaty, and (d) our business obligations such as a formal contract to perform certain tasks or a tacit contract to treat our employees decently. The Muslim must curb his free will to act according to the moral code laid out by Allah.

From an economics standpoint, Islam rejects the principle of *laissez-faire* and the Western reliance on the concept of the "Invisible Hand."[76] Since a key part of the make-up of man is the *nafs ammārah*, he is prone to abuse such a system. The examples of Ivan Boesky, Michael Milken and the junk bonds fiasco, the Savings and Loan scandal in the United States, the BCCI debacle, the corruptive practices of the government and the Mafia in Italy, the *baqshīsh* system in the Middle East, the stock market scandals in

---

[73] *Qur'an* 18:29.
[74] Maudoodī, p. 4.
[75] *Qur'an* 5:1.
[76] Naqvi, pp. 66-67.

Japan, etc., all demonstrate the deficiencies in the capitalistic system. *Homo Islamicus*[77] guided by Allah's law will consciously choose to be ethical.

Responsibility

Unlimited freedom is absurd; it implies no responsibility or accountability. To meet the dictates of *'adl* and unity that we see in Allah's creation, man needs to be accountable for his actions. Allah stresses this concept of moral responsibility for one's actions:

> *[...]Whoever works evil, will be requited accordingly. Nor will he find, besides Allah, any protector or helper. If any do deeds of righteousness—be they male or female—and have faith, they will enter heaven, and not the least injustice will be done to them.*[78]

Islam is fair: as previously discussed, a person is not responsible for his/her actions (a) if he/she has not reached the age of puberty, (b) if he/she is insane or (c) if he/she is acting during sleep.

Within the concept of responsibility, Islam draws a distinction between *farḍ al 'ayn* (individual responsibility that is non-transferable) and *farḍ al kifāyah* (collective responsibility dischargeable by a few).[79] For example, *farḍ al kifāyah* suggests that if someone is able to earn a suitable living and wants to occupy himself by studying some of the religious sciences but finds that his work will not allow him to do so, then he may be given zakat since seeking knowledge is considered a collective duty. As for one who is engaged in supererogatory worship (*nawāfil*) or for one who occupies himself in *nawāfil* with no time to pursue his own livelihood, he may not receive zakat. This is because the benefit of his worship is confined to him alone, contrary to the one who seeks knowledge. *Farḍ al 'ayn*, however, means an injunction or ordinance unconditional in its nature, and general in its application, and the obligation of which extends alike to every individual. Thus fasting and prayer are of the class *farḍ al 'ayn*, and a Muslim cannot shift his personal responsibility for praying.[80]

---

[77] Zarqa, M. A., "Social Welfare Function and Consumer Behavior: An Islamic Formulation of Selected Issues." Paper presented at the First International Conference on Islamic Economics, Makkah, 1976.

[78] *Qur'an* 4:123-124.

[79] Ahmad, Khurshid. Foreword in Naqvi, pp. 14.

[80] *Al Hidāyah*, Vol. II (Ḥanafi Manual), Chapter I, Serial No. 3988.

Responsibility in Islam is multi-layered and focuses at both the micro- (individual) level and the macro- (organizational and societal) level. Responsibility in Islam even brings together both the micro and the macro levels (e.g., between the individual and various societal institutions and forces). As Sayed Kotb points out,

> *Islam lays down the principle of mutual responsibility in all its various shapes and forms. In it we find the responsibilities which exist between a man and his soul, between a man and his immediate family, between the individual and society, between community and other communities. [...]*[81]

We shall discuss later this expanded meaning of responsibility with specific reference to the social responsibility of organizations.

Application of the Responsibility Axiom to Business Ethics. Should a Muslim business person behave unethically, he cannot blame his actions on the pressures of business or on the fact that everybody else is behaving unethically. He bears the ultimate responsibility for his own actions. Accordingly, Allah states:

> *Every soul will be (held) in pledge for its deeds.*[82]

Hence, this axiom ties in with the other axioms of unity, equilibrium and free will. All obligations must be honored unless morally wrong. For example, Abraham (saaw) rejected his filial obligations because his father wanted him to engage in *shirk* or idolatry. On the other hand, the Prophet (saaw) observed the conditions of the treaty of Hudhaybīyah although it meant that Abū Jandal, a new Muslim, had to be returned to the Quraysh envoys. Once a Muslim has given his word or engaged in a legitimate contract, he must see it through.

> *The Prophet (peace be upon him) said, "The signs of a hypocrite are three: 1. Whenever he speaks, he tells a lie. 2. Whenever he promises, he always breaks it (his promise). 3. If you trust him,*

---

[81] Kotb, p. 56.

[82] *Qur'an* 74:38.

he proves to be dishonest (if you keep something as a trust with him, he will not return it)."[83]

Benevolence

Benevolence (*iḥsān*) or kindness to others is defined as "an act which benefits persons other than those from whom the act proceeds without any obligation."[84] Kindness is encouraged in Islam. The Prophet (saaw) is reported to have said:

> *The inmates of Paradise are of three types: one who wields authority and is just and fair; one who is truthful and has been endowed with power to do good deeds; and the person who is merciful and kind-hearted towards his relatives and to every pious Muslim, and who does not stretch out his hand in spite of having a large family to support.*[85]

Application of the Benevolence Axiom to Business Ethics. According to al Ghazzālī,[86] there are six kinds of benevolence:

1. If a person needs a thing, one should give it to him, making as little profit as possible. If the giver forgoes the profit, it will be better for him.
2. If a man purchases anything from a poor person, it will be more graceful on his part to suffer a little loss by paying him more than what he considers to be the proper price. Such an act must produce an ennobling effect, and a contrary act is likely to have the reverse effect. It is not praiseworthy to pay a rich man more than his due when he is notorious for charging high rates of profit.
3. In realizing one's dues and loans one must act benevolently by giving the debtors more time to pay than is due and, if necessary, one should make reductions in loans to provide relief to the debtors.
4. It is only proper that people who want to return the goods they have purchased should be permitted to do so as a matter of benevolence.
5. It is a graceful act on the part of a debtor if he pays his debts without being asked to do so, if possible long before they are due.

---

[83] Abū Hurayrah, *Ṣaḥīḥ al Bukhārī*, hadith no. 1.32.
[84] See Umar-ud-din, p. 241.
[85] Iyād Ibn Himar, *Ṣaḥīḥ Muslim*, hadith no. 6853.
[86] See Umar-ud-din, pp. 241-242.

6. When selling things on credit one should be generous enough, not to press for payment when people are not able to pay on the stipulated terms.

Although the above axioms guide us in our day to day behavior, they are more descriptive of the ethical philosophy of Islam. The Qur'an and the Sunnah complement these axioms by specifying the degree of lawfulness of key types of behaviors as well as the *ḥarām* and *ḥalāl* business areas for Muslim businessmen.

Degrees of Lawful and Unlawful Behavior in Islam[87]

In describing the moral code of Islam, it is important to for us to understand that actions can be categorized according to their degree of lawfulness or unlawfulness. In *fiqh*, five such classes have been enunciated.

1. **Farḍ** represents the class of actions that is mandatory on every person claiming to be a Muslim. For example, praying *ṣalāt* five times a day, fasting, zakah are among the compulsory actions that a Muslim must perform.
2. **Mustaḥabb** describes the class of actions that are not obligatory but highly recommended of Muslims. Example of such actions would include supererogatory fasting beyond Ramadan, praying the *nawāfil* prayers, etc.
3. **Mubāḥ** actions are permissible in the sense they are specified neither as mandatory nor as forbidden. For example, a Muslim may like a certain type of *ḥalāl* food over another type of *ḥalāl* food. Or a Muslim may like gardening.
4. **Makrūḥ** actions are not absolutely forbidden, but are detested. The *makrūḥ* is less in degree than the *ḥarām*, and the punishment for *makrūḥ* is less than for those acts which are *ḥarām*, except when done in excess and in a manner leading towards what is *ḥarām*.[88] For example, although smoking is not expressly forbidden like drinking alcohol, it is in itself a action that is *makrūḥ*.
5. **Ḥarām** actions are unlawful and prohibited. Committing them is a major sin, e.g., murder, adultery, drinking alcohol. Such acts are likely to incur the punishment of Allah in the Hereafter as well as a legal punishment in this world.[89]

---

[87] Badawi, Gamal, loc. cit.
[88] Al Qaraḍāwī, p. 10.
[89] Loc. cit.

Interestingly, relatively few things fall under the category of *ḥarām* or *ḥalāl*. The boundaries between the five above-mentioned categories are not absolute. For example, what is *ḥarām* under one set of circumstances may become permissible under others. Thus, a Muslim is not allowed to eat pork. However, should he fear death from starvation, and nothing but pork is available, he is allowed to eat pork in that specific situation.[90]

Table 3 summarizes the Islamic principles pertaining to *ḥalāl* and *ḥarām* as presented by Yūsuf al Qaraḍāwī. Based upon the above categorization and principles 4 and 5, a first rule is that what is lawful is also wholesome and pure. What is not lawful can hurt us. For example, Islam has long discouraged Muslims from drinking alcohol. It is only recently that childbirth studies have indicated that any amount of alcohol consumed by a woman during pregnancy can affect the child in her womb, and lead to fetal alcohol syndrome and/or mental retardation. Implicitly, what is lawful is also moral, and what is unlawful is immoral. For example, adultery is both unlawful and immoral. A second rule is that what leads to an unlawful act is also unlawful. Hence, pornography is unlawful and immoral because it may lead to adultery.

In mapping out one's ethical behavior, it is very important for Muslims both to avoid the unlawful and to avoid making the unlawful as lawful. Allah Himself says:

> *Say: See you what things Allah has sent down to you for sustenance? Yet you hold forbidden some things thereof and (some things) lawful. Say: Has Allah indeed permitted you, or do you invent (things) to attribute to Allah?*[91]

The reverse is also true.[92] Muslims should not make unlawful what Allah has labeled as lawful. For example, a buffalo may be an endangered species. One may stop hunting it in order to allow its herds to grow back, but one cannot say that it is forbidden to eat buffalo meat or to trade in buffalo skins.

---

[90] Al Kaysī, Marwān Ibrāhīm. *Morals and Manners in Islam*. Leicester, UK: The Islamic Foundation, 1989, p. 50.

[91] *Qur'an* 10:59.

[92] *Qur'an* 5:87.

Ḥalāl and *Ḥarām* Business Areas

By virtue of rules 4 and 6 above, what is *ḥarām* may be presumed to correlate with business areas that are themselves *ḥarām* and hence unethical. Similarly, what is *ḥalāl* may be presumed to correlate with business areas that are themselves *ḥalāl* and ethical.

Ḥalāl Earnings

Islam, through the example of the Prophet (saaw) and the rightly-guided Caliphs, demonstrates the importance of trade or business. Abū Bakr (raa) ran a cloth business, 'Umar (raa) had a corn trading business, and 'Uthmān (raa) also had a cloth business. The Anṣār among the Companions of the Prophet (may Allah be pleased with them) engaged in farming. In fact, except for the trades that have been prohibited (see below and other sources such as al Qaraḍāwī), Islam actively encourages Muslims to get involved in business and commerce:

> *Allah's Messenger (peace be upon him) was asked what type of earning was best and replied, "A man's work with his hand and every business transaction which is approved."*[93]

Table 3 Islamic Principles Pertaining *Ḥalāl* and *Ḥarām*[94]	
1.	The basic principle is the permissibility of things.
2.	To make lawful and to prohibit is the right of Allah alone.
3.	Prohibiting the *ḥalāl* and permitting the *ḥarām* is similar to committing *shirk*.
4.	The prohibition of things is due to their impurity and harmfulness.
5.	What is *ḥalāl* is sufficient, while what is *ḥarām* is superfluous.
6.	Whatever is conducive to the *ḥarām* is itself *ḥarām*.
7.	Falsely representing the *ḥarām* as *ḥalāl* is prohibited.
8.	Good intentions do not make the *ḥarām* acceptable.
9.	Doubtful things are to be avoided.
10.	The *ḥarām* is prohibited to everyone alike.
11.	Necessity dictates exceptions.

[93] Rāfi' ibn Khadīj, *Mishkāt al Maṣābīḥ*, hadith no. 2783.
[94] Al Qaraḍāwī, p. 11.

Earning money through a *ḥalāl* trade is vastly preferred over begging. This principle is emphasized in the following hadith:

> *A man of the Anṣār came to the Prophet (peace be upon him) and begged from him. He (the Prophet) asked, "Have you nothing in your house?" He replied, "Yes, a piece of cloth, a part of which we wear and a part of which we spread (on the ground), and a wooden bowl from which we drink water."*
>
> *He said, "Bring them to me." He then brought these articles to him and he (the Prophet) took them in his hands and asked, "Who will buy these?" A man said, "I shall buy them for one dirham." He said twice or thrice, "Who will offer more than one dirham?" A man said, "I shall buy them for two dirhams."*
>
> *He gave these to him and took the two dirhams and, giving them to the Anṣārī, he said, "Buy food with one of them and hand it to your family, and buy an ax and bring it to me." He then brought it to him. The Apostle of Allah (peace be upon him) fixed a handle on it with his own hands and said, "Go, gather firewood and sell it, and do not let me see you for a fortnight." The man went away and gathered firewood and sold it. When he had earned ten dirhams, he came to him and bought a garment with some of them and food with the others.*
>
> *The Apostle of Allah (peace be upon him) then said, "This is better for you than that begging should come as a spot on your face on the Day of Judgment. Begging is right only for three people: one who is in grinding poverty, one who is seriously in debt, or one who is responsible for compensation and finds it difficult to pay."*[95]

Work in Agriculture

Allah describes in the Qur'an the processes underlying agriculture and farming: how rain is sent down and flows throughout the earth, making it fertile and ready for cultivating; how the winds play a role in scattering seeds, and how crops grow.

---

[95] Anas ibn Mālik, Abū Dāwūd, hadith no. 1637.

It is He Who has spread out the earth for (His) creatures: Therein is fruit and date palms, producing spathes (enclosing dates): Also corn, with (its) leaves and stalk for fodder and sweet-smelling plants. Then which of the favors of your Lord will you deny?[96]

This Qur'anic verse and many others[97] provide motivation for agricultural work. Al Qaraḍāwī also mentions the following hadith in support of agricultural work:

Allah's Messenger (peace be upon him) said, "There is none amongst the Muslims who plants a tree or sows seeds, and then a bird, or a person or an animal eats from it, but is regarded as a charitable gift for him."[98]

Work in Industry and Professional Areas

Besides agriculture, Muslims are encouraged to develop proficiency in industries, crafts and professions that are instrumental to the survival and betterment of the community. In fact, development of these skills represent a *farḍ kifāyah*. Imām al Ghazzālī stresses this point:

Sciences whose knowledge is deemed farḍ kifāyah *comprise every area which is indispensable for the welfare of this world.*[99]

Many professions that are ordinarily looked down upon have been given dignity by Islam. For example, Moses (saw) worked as a hired hand for eight years to gain the hand of his future wife. The Prophet (saaw) also worked as a shepherd for several years:

The Messenger of Allah, may Allah bless him and grant him peace, said, "There is no prophet who has not herded sheep," and someone asked, "You as well, Messenger of Allah?" He said, "Myself as well."[100]

---

[96] *Qur'an* 55:10-13.
[97] *Qur'an* 71:19-20; 80:24-28; 15:19-22.
[98] Anas ibn Mālik, *Ṣaḥīḥ al Bukhārī*, 3.513.
[99] Al Ghazzālī. *The Book of Knowledge*. Lahore, Pakistan: Sh. Muhammad Ashraf. Translated by Nabih Amin Faris, p. 37. The above quote was cited in al Qaraḍāwī, pp. 131-132.
[100] Mālik ibn Anas, *al Muwaṭṭa'*, 54.6.18.

In general, then, Islam looks on work which fills a *ḥalāl* need in society as good provided that the person performs it in an Islamic manner.

Ḥarām Earnings

A partial list of businesses that Muslims should stay away from is included below.

Trading in Alcohol. Alcohol consumption and trade is prohibited:

> *Truly, Allah has cursed* khamr *and has cursed the one who produces it, the one for whom it is produced, the one who drinks it, the one who serves it, the one who carries it, the one for whom it is carried, the one who sells it, the one who earns from the sale of it, the one who buys it, and the one for whom it is bought.*[101]

Hence, a Muslim businessman cannot run any trade which imports or exports alcoholic beverages; he cannot own any business where alcohol is sold, nor can he work in any such business.

Drug Dealing and Trading. Yūsuf al Qaraḍāwī classifies drugs such as marijuana, cocaine, opium and the like under the prohibited category of *khamr*.[102] The criterion for defining what is *khamr* comes from 'Umar ibn al Khaṭṭāb:

> *Khamr is what befogs the mind.*

Muslim jurists, including Ibn Taymīyah, have unanimously prohibited such drugs because of their intoxicating and hallucinogenic effects. Their use may result in evil behavior and have harmful effects upon the person using the substance. Al Qaraḍāwī cites a verse from the Qur'an:

> *And do not kill yourselves; indeed, Allah is ever merciful to you.*[103]

---

[101] Reported by al Tirmidhī and Ibn Mājah, on reliable authority in al Qaraḍāwī, p. 74.
[102] Ibid., p. 76.
[103] *Qur'an* 4:29.

Based upon the general ruling about trading in *khamr*, such businesses that involve drugs in any aspect of its trade are not permissible to Muslims.

Sculptors and Artists. Following the rule that something that leads to a forbidden thing is also forbidden,[104] businesses involving the manufacture of pictures, statues, etc., as objects of worship or as objects to be likened to Allah's creations are clearly forbidden in Islam. In a hadith narrated by 'Ā'ishah (raa),

> *Allah's Apostle (peace be upon him) returned from a journey when I had placed a curtain of mine having pictures over (the door of) one of my rooms. When Allah's Apostle (peace be upon him) saw it, he tore it and said, "The people who will receive the severest punishment on the Day of Resurrection will be those who try to make the likeness of Allah's creations." So we turned it (i.e., the curtain) into one or two cushions.*[105]

Production and Sale of *Ḥarām* Goods. As can be seen from the prohibitions regarding *khamr*, trading in goods used for committing sins is *ḥarām*, e.g., pornography, hashish and the like, idol manufacturing, etc. Such trade tends to promote and propagate what is *ḥarām* and may encourage *ḥarām* behavior. The Prophet (peace be on him) said,

> *Allah and His Apostle made illegal the trade of alcohol, dead animals, pigs and idols.*[106]

Prostitution. Although legal in many countries, Islam prohibits this trade. In fact, when Islam came, it put an end to the exploitation of women used in this fashion. The following hadith and Qur'anic citation strongly condemn prostitution:

> *'Abd Allāh ibn Ubayy ibn Salūl used to say to his slave girl: "Go and fetch something for us by committing prostitution." It was in this connection that Allah, the Exalted and Glorious, revealed this verse: "And compel not your slave-girls to prostitution when they desire to keep chaste in order to seek the frail*

---

[104] Principle number 5, in al Qaraḍāwī, *Al Ḥalāl wa al Ḥarām fi al Islām*, p. 11.
[105] 'Ā'ishah (raa), in *Ṣaḥīḥ al Bukhārī*, hadith no. 7.838.
[106] Jābir ibn 'Abd Allāh, in *Ṣaḥīḥ al Bukhārī*, hadith no. 3.438.

> *goods of this world's life, and whoever compels them, then surely after their compulsion Allah is Forgiving, Merciful."* (24:33).[107]

Al Gharar. The Prophet (saaw) forbade any kind of trade involving uncertainty, regarding an unspecified quantity to be exchanged or delivered. Futures trading is therefore prohibited in Islam. It involves the selling of commodities not yet in the possession of the seller, the selling of animals still unborn, the selling of agricultural produce not yet harvested, etc.[108]

> *The Messenger of Allah, may Allah bless him and grant him peace, forbade selling fruit until it had started to ripen. He forbade the transaction to both buyer and seller.*[109]

Not every sale involving uncertainty is prohibited.[110] For example, a person may purchase a house without knowing what is inside its walls. What is prohibited are sales where there is an obvious element of uncertainty that may lead to dispute, conflict or the unfair impoundment of one's money. Sales where the element of uncertainty is minimal are permissible.

Prohibited Form of Sharecropping. Sharecropping is allowed under certain circumstances and disallowed under others. Let us assume a situation where a landowner lends his land to another person to cultivate. The cultivator can use his own equipment, seeds and animals provided he gets a specified percentage of the produce from the land. The owner may also furnish the cultivator with seeds, equipment and animals. This type of sharecropping is allowed. The Prophet (saaw) provided the people of Khaybar with land to cultivate in return for half of the produce.[111] A second type of sharecropping called *mukhābarah* is disallowed. In this case, the owner asks for a specified weight or measure of the grain produced and the cultivator is supposed to receive the remainder of the harvest. Should the land be partly productive, the cultivator may receive nothing. This is why the Prophet (saaw) required that both parties share the total produce however much or little it may be, and forbade this type of practice. The following hadith narrated by Rāfi' ibn Khadīj supports this point.

---

[107] Jābir ibn 'Abd Allāh, in *Ṣaḥīḥ Muslim,* hadith no. 7180.

[108] Gani, pp. 6-7, and al Qaraḍāwī, pp. 253-254.

[109] 'Abd Allāh ibn 'Umar, *àl Muwaṭṭa'*, hadith no. 31.8.10.

[110] Al Qaraḍāwī, p. 254.

[111] 'Abd Allāh ibn 'Umar, *Ṣaḥīḥ al Bukhārī*, hadith no. 3.485.

We worked on farms more than anybody else in Madinah. We used to rent the land at the yield of specific delimited portion of it to be given to the landlord. Sometimes the vegetation of that portion was affected by blights etc., while the rest remained safe and vice versa. So the Prophet (peace be upon him) forbade this practice. At that time gold or silver were not used (for renting the land).[112]

The prohibition of the second type of sharecropping illustrates Islam's preoccupation with the axioms of balance and benevolence. Both the land owner and the cultivator must behave equitably: the landowner must not exact too high a portion of the produce, and the cultivator must look after the land judiciously. Both parties share in the gain and loss. This is clearly more fair than leasing where the landlord collects his rent no matter what, and the tenant may or may harvest any produce.[113]

For businesses not mentioned above, it is imperative that the reader consults with Muslims that are qualified jurists.

Developing an Ethical Organizational Climate

Ethical or unethical conduct does not take place in a void. They usually take place within an organizational context that facilitates their occurrence. The actions of other organizational participants as well as the norms and values embodied within the firm's culture may add to the ethical climate within the organization. The English proverb "birds of a feather flock together" is applicable here. The Serpeco scandal took place when New York City policemen decided that taking bribes was an easy way to make extra money. Before long, the whole department was almost totally corrupt. The Milken, Levine and Boesky scandals are all incidents where organizational participants flouted ethics because supervision was either too lax or they believed that the law would never catch them. For his misdeeds, Michael Milken had to pay a fine of over $500 million and spend time in jail.

In examining the ethical climate in an organization, one needs to start with the individual's own ethical stance. Some are committed to ethical behavior, and will not engage in doubtful practices. Others are influenced by the unethical standards of their peers or boss or by external environmental pressures. For example, employees in hypercompetitive industries may feel

---

[112] Rāfi' ibn Khadīj, *Ṣaḥīḥ al Bukhārī*, hadith no. 3.520.

[113] Ibn Taymīyah. 1992. *Public Duties in Islam: The Institution of the Ḥisbah*. Leicester, UK: The Islamic Foundation, p. 41.

compelled to excel by whatever means possible and may resort to unethical behavior, such as Boesky's insider trading activities, in order to obtain a competitive advantage. Should a manager become cognizant of unethical behavior and do nothing about it, he or she is in fact signaling that such practices are tolerated. At other times, organizations may unintentionally encourage unethical behavior by their reward system. For example, Eastern Airlines gave a bonus to their mechanics to encourage them to get airplanes back into circulation as fast as possible. Thus, airplanes that did not receive adequate maintenance were flying when they should not have.

The rash of recent scandals on Wall Street, in the savings and loan industry in the United States and in other countries' business sector has incited many firms to re-examine their ethical standards. This renewed concern with ethics can be more clearly understood by discussing organizations' social responsibility with respect to their multiple stakeholders.

An Islamic Perspective of the Social Responsibility of Organizations

Social responsibility refers to the "obligations that an organization has to protect and contribute to the society in which it functions."[114] An organization exercises social responsibility in three domains: its stakeholders, the natural environment, and the general social welfare.

Organizational Stakeholders

Organizational stakeholders represent the people and/or organizations that are affected by the actions of an organization. Some of the key organizational stakeholders are included in Table 4. Ethics can influence how the firm relates to its employees, how employees relate to the firm, and how the firm relates to other economic agents.

Relationship of the Firm to Its Employees

In non-Islamic arenas, ethical standards are often dictated by the behavior of managers. These standards cover hiring and firing, wages, sexual harassment, and other areas relevant to one's working conditions.

---

[114] Barney and Griffin, p. 726.

Table 4 Key Ethical Focus Areas[115]		
Focus Areas	Stakeholder(s)	Issues
Relationship of the firm to its employees	Employees	Hiring and firing; Wages and working condition; Privacy
Relationship of employees to the firm	Firm	Conflicts of interest; Secrecy; Honesty; Skills training and qualifications
Relationship of firm to key stakeholders	Suppliers	Cost of Inputs
	Buyers	Hoarding and price manipulation; quantity and quality of goods sold; selling strategy; use of *ribā* in financing sales.
	Debtors	Repayment terms
	General Public	Hoarding; abuse of environment
	Stockholders/Owners/ Partners	Distribution of losses/gains
	The needy	*Ṣadaqah*
	Competitors	Fair competition

Hiring, Promotion and Other Employee-related Decisions. Islam wishes us to treat all Muslims equally well. For example, in hiring, promoting or any other decision where a manager is evaluating one person's performance against another's, fairness and justice (*'adl*) are a must. Allah directs us to do so:

> *Allah commands you to render back your trusts to those whom they are due; and when you judge between man and man, that you judge with justice.*[116]

Fair Wages: Ibn Taymīyah suggests that an employer is under obligation to pay a fair remuneration to his employees. Some employers may take advantage of a worker and underpay him or her because of their need for

[115] Barney, Jay B. & Griffin, Ricky W. *The Management of Organizations.* © 1992 by Houghton Mifflin Company, Table 22.1, p. 722.. Adapted with permission.
[116] *Qur'an* 4:58.

income. Islam is against such exploitation. If the wage level is too low, the individual may not feel motivated to put in an adequate amount of effort. Similarly if the wage level is too high, the employer may not be able to make a profit and keep the business going. In an Islamic organizations, wages must be set in an equitable manner both with respect to employees and the employer. On the Day of Judgment, the Prophet (saaw) will be a witness against "one who employs a laborer and gets the full work done by him but does not pay him his wages."[117] The emphasis on wage equity has permeated Islamic history for centuries. During the time of the four rightly-guided Caliphs and until the advent of Western colonialism, the institution of the *ḥisbah* was developed to uphold public law and order and oversee the relationship between buyers and sellers in the market. The mission of the *ḥisbah* was to safeguard right conduct and guard against dishonesty. The *hisba* was under the guidance of the *muḥtasib* who was responsible "for the maintenance of public morality and economic ethics."[118] One of the duties of the *muḥtasib* was to arbitrate in dispute over wages. In such cases, the *muḥtasib* would often propose the *ujrat al mithl* (wage acceptable for a similar work by others) as an equitable wage.[119] This is an example of the principle of equity or justice at work again.

Respect for Employee's Beliefs. The general principle of *tawḥīd* or unity applies to all aspects of the relationship between a firm and its employees. Muslim businessmen should not treat their employees as though Islam is inconsequential during business hours. For example, Muslim employees should be given time off for prayers, should not be coerced into acting against the Islamic moral code, should be given respite if they are sick and cannot perform, and should not be harassed sexually or otherwise. To foster equity and balance, non-Muslim employees' beliefs should be similarly respected.

> *Allah forbids you not, with regard to those who fight you not for (your) faith nor drive you out of your homes, from dealing kindly and justly with them: For Allah loves those who are just.*[120]

---

[117] Abū Hurayrah, *Ṣaḥīḥ al Bukhārī*, hadith no. 3.430.

[118] Ahmad, Khurshid. Preface to Ibn Taymīyah's *Public Duties in Islam*, pp. 6-7.

[119] Khan, M. A, "Al Ḥisbah and the Islamic Economy." Paper published in the appendix to Ibn Taymīyah's *Public Duties in Islam*, pp. 135-150.

[120] *Qur'an* 60:8.

Accountability. Although both the employer and employee can willfully cheat each other behind each other's back, they are both accountable for their actions in front of Allah. For example, the Prophet (saaw) never used to withhold the wages of any person.[121]

Right to Privacy. If an employee has a physical problem which prevents him or her from performing certain tasks or if an employee has committed a blunder in the past, the employer must not publicize it. This would breach the privacy of the employee.

> *Whether you publish a good deed or conceal it or cover evil with pardon verily Allah doth blot out (sins) and hath power (in the judgment of values).*[122]

Benevolence. The principle of benevolence (*iḥsān*) should permeate the relationship between business and employee. At times, the business may not be doing well, and the employee may have to endure a temporary reduction in his wages for the same amount of work hours. Another aspect of benevolence is not to place undue pressure on employees to conform blindly. A recent survey of 1,227 *Harvard Business Review* readers revealed that superiors often placed pressure on their subordinates to sign false documents, disregard superiors' mistakes, and conduct business with friends of their bosses. When faced with pressure from above, employees feel compelled to compromise their integrity.

Relationship of Employees to the Firm

Many ethical issues characterize the relationship of the employee to the firm, especially with respect to honesty, secrecy, and conflicts of interest. Thus, an employee must neither embezzle the funds of the company, not reveal company secrets to outsiders. Another unethical practice occurs when managers add false charges for meals and other services to their company expense accounts. Some of them cheat because they feel underpaid, and wish to restore equity. At other times, it is pure greed. For example, Albert Miano who embezzled $1 million from his employer admitted that his primary motivator was greed.[123] For Muslim employees, Allah gives them a clear warning in the Qur'an:

---

[121] Anas ibn Mālik, *Ṣaḥīḥ al Bukhārī*, hadith no. 3.480.
[122] *Qur'an* 4:149.
[123] *Fortune*, April 25, 1988.

Say: "The things that my Lord hath indeed forbidden are: shameful deeds whether open or secret; sins and trespasses against truth or reason;"[124]

Muslim employees, cognizant of the above *āyāt*, should never intentionally act in an unethical manner.

Good intentions may yet be derailed by ambiguous situations and perceptual traps. Surveys of sales personnel have indicated that employees sometimes find themselves in ambiguous situations where there are no definite ethical guidelines. For example, a supplier may invite a sales person to lunch in the hope of getting more slack on a credit sale. Should the sales person accept to go out to a business luncheon or should he insist on paying for his food? Would he offend his client? In this situation, the sales person may experience greater difficulty in making the right decision because employees often view themselves as more ethical than their peers. As a result, they may condone going to a business luncheon with a client on the basis that this is a commonly accepted business practice. To avoid potential employee misconduct, Islamic organizations need to go one step further, and develop an explicit code of ethics.

Relationship of the Firm to Other Stakeholders

A firm exists in a web of relationships with a whole array of stakeholders. These include: suppliers, buyers, customers, unions, government agencies and competitors. Table 4 summarizes the key focus areas and the issues pertinent to them.

Suppliers. When dealing with suppliers, business ethics suggest that one should negotiate a fair price, and not take advantage of one's bigger size or clout. To avoid any future misunderstanding, Allah has enjoined us to put contractual obligations in writing.

O you who believe! When you deal with each other in transactions involving future obligations in a fixed period of time, reduce them to writing. [...] Let him who incurs the liability dictate, but let him fear His Lord Allah, and not diminish aught of what he owes. [...][125]

---

[124] *Qur'an* 7:33.
[125] *Qur'an* 2:282.

As explained earlier, *gharar* types of transactions are also explicitly forbidden between the firm and its suppliers.

> *In the time of Marwān ibn al Ḥakam, receipts were given to people for the produce of the market at al Jār. People bought and sold the receipts among themselves before they took delivery of the goods. Zayd ibn Thābit and one of the Companions of the Messenger of Allah, may Allah bless him and grant him peace, went to Marwān ibn al Ḥakam and said, "Marwān! Do you make usury* ḥalāl*?" He said, "I seek refuge with Allah! What is that?" He said, "These receipts which people buy and sell before they take delivery of the goods." Marwān therefore sent a guard to follow them and to take them from people's hands and return them to their owners.*[126]

Despite the permissibility of agency in general, merchants are prohibited from interfering with the free market system through a specific type of brokering. This type of brokering may lead to price inflation. Let us take the example of a farmer going to the marketplace in a town to sell some of his goods. A townsman may approach the farmer, asking that the goods be left with him for a while until the prices go up. If the farmer had sold the goods without the interference of the townsman, the public would have purchased them at the current lower price; both the public and the farmer would have benefited. However, when the townsman stores the goods until prices increase and then sell them, the public has to pay more, and the broker makes excess profits. This type of brokering is forbidden.

> *Allah's Messenger (peace be upon him) said: "The townsman should not sell for a man from the desert; leave the people alone; Allah will give them provision from one another."*[127]

Al Qaraḍāwī, however, points out that brokerage is generally permissible except when there is interference in the free market system—as in the case just cited. There is nothing wrong with the broker's charging a fee for his services. This fee may be a fixed amount or proportional to the volume of sales or whatever is agreed among the parties involved.[128]

---

[126] Zayd ibn Thābit, *al Muwaṭṭa'*, hadith no. 31.19.44.
[127] Jābir ibn 'Abd Allāh, *Ṣaḥīḥ Muslim*, hadith no. 3630.
[128] Al Qaraḍāwī, pp. 258-259.

Buyers/Consumers. Buyers should expect to receive goods that are in working conditions and priced fairly. They should also be notified of any deficiencies. Islam forbids the following practices when dealing with consumers or buyers:

- Use of incorrect weights and measures. In the story of Shu'ayb, Allah says:

  Give just measure, and cause no loss (to others by fraud). And weigh with scales true and upright. And withhold not things justly due to men, [...].[129]

  The Muslim businessman should not demand honesty from others while being himself dishonest. In other words, the Islamic moral code applies to all equally.
- Hoarding and price manipulation. As Sheikh al Qaraḍāwī points out, the market system is free in Islam, and is allowed to respond to supply and demand.[130] However, Islam does not tolerate interference in the market system by hoarding or other forms of price manipulation. Allah's Messenger (peace be upon him) said:

  He who hoards is a sinner.[131]

  In cases where businessmen are engaging in hoarding and other forms of price manipulation, Islam allows price control in order to meet the needs of society and to provide protection against greed. However, if a commodity is being sold without any hoarding, and its price rises because of natural shortages or scarcity or an increase in demand, then this circumstance is due to Allah. Businessmen cannot then be compelled to sell at a fixed price.[132]
- Adulterated or spoiled products. Islam prohibits any kind of fraudulent transaction whether during a purchase or a sale. The Muslim businessman must be honest at all times. The following hadith exemplifies how the Islamic moral code views deceptive business practices:

---

[129] *Qur'an* 26:181-183.
[130] Al Qaraḍāwī, pp. 255-257.
[131] Ma'mar ibn 'Abd Allāh al 'Adawī, *Ṣaḥīḥ Muslim*, hadith no. 3910.
[132] Al Qaraḍāwī, p. 256.

The Messenger of Allah (peace be upon him) happened to pass by a heap of eatables (corn). He thrust his hand in that (heap) and his fingers were moistened. He said to the owner of the heap of eatables (corn), "What is this?" "Messenger of Allah, these have been drenched by rainfall." He (the Prophet) remarked, "Why did you not place this (the drenched part of the heap) over other eatables so that the people could see it? He who deceives is not of me (is not my follower)."[133]

A similar situation took place when 'Umar ibn al Khaṭṭāb punished a man who was selling milk diluted with water. 'Umar spilled the man's milk not because it was unfit for drinking, but rather because the buyer would not know the relative quantities of milk and water.[134] Hence, Islam encourages Muslim businessmen to be forthright, and reveal any defects prior to a sale. Should either party then decide that they do not wish to participate in the contract, they may do so.

The Prophet (peace be upon him) said, "Both the buyer and the seller have the option of canceling or confirming the bargain unless they separate."[135]

In the case of perishables, the buyer is entitled to a full refund of the purchase price should the goods purchased prove unfit for use.

If a person purchase eggs, musk melons, cucumbers, walnuts, or the like, and after opening them discover them to be of bad quality; in that case, if they be altogether unfit for use, the purchaser is entitled to complete restitution of the price from the seller, as the sale is invalid, because of the subject of it not being in reality property.[136]

- Swearing to support a sale. When engaged in deceiving a buyer, the sin resulting from this deception is increased if the businessman validates his sales pitch through false oaths.

---

133 Abū Hurayrah, *Ṣaḥīḥ Muslim*, hadith no. 0183.

134 Ibn Taymīyah, p. 65.

135 Ḥakīm ibn Ḥizām, *Ṣaḥīḥ al Bukhārī*, hadith no. 3.327.

136 *Al Hidāyah* (Ḥanafī manual), vol. II, 4440.

I heard Allah's Messenger (peace be upon him) saying, "The swearing (by the seller) may persuade the buyer to purchase the goods but that will be deprived of Allah's blessing."[137]

- Purchase of stolen property. The Muslim businessman must not knowingly purchase stolen property either for himself or for future resale. By so doing, he sanctions the crime of the robber. The Prophet (saaw) said,

He who buys the stolen property, with the knowledge that it was stolen, shares in the sin and shame of stealing.[138]

Further, the passage of time does not make a *ḥarām* piece of property *ḥalāl*. The original owner of the stolen goods retains his right on it.

- Prohibition of interest or *ribā*. Although Islam encourages businessmen to augment their capital through trade, it explicitly prohibits them from capital expansion through lending on interest. The size of the rate of interest charged is inconsequential; *ribā* is absolutely prohibited. There is no opportunity cost of lending money in Islam. The lender is making money without any fear of loss. Further, since the lender is likely to be wealthy and the borrower poor, *ribā* simply increases the gap between the haves and the have-nots. Islam encourages the circulation of wealth. Allah states in the Qur'an:

Those who devour usury will not stand except as stands one whom The Evil One by his touch has driven to madness. That is because they say: "Trade is like usury," but Allah has permitted trade and forbidden usury.[139]

The sin of dealing with *ribā* affects all the parties involved in a *ribā* transaction:

Allah's Messenger (peace be upon him) cursed the acceptor of interest and its payer, and one who records it, and the two witnesses; and he said, "They are all equal."[140]

---

[137] Abū Hurayrah, *Ṣaḥīḥ al Bukhārī*, hadith no. 3.300.

[138] Reported by al Bayhaqī and cited in al Qaraḍāwī.

[139] *Qur'an* 2:275.

[140] Jābir ibn 'Abd Allāh, *Ṣaḥīḥ Muslim*, hadith no. 3881.

Debtors. In general, Islam encourages benevolence. If any debtor is in financial trouble, Allah encourages kindness:

> *If the debtor is in a difficulty, grant him time till it is easy for him to repay. But if you remit it by way of charity, that is best for you if you only knew.*[141]

In fact, a hadith of the Prophet (saaw) reaffirms the importance of magnanimity on the part of the lender.

> *The Prophet (peace be upon him) said, "Before your time the angels received the soul of a man and asked him, 'Did you do any good deeds (in your life)?' He replied, 'I used to order my employees to grant time to the rich person to pay his debts at his convenience and excuse (the one in hard circumstances).' So Allah said to the angels, 'Excuse him.'"*[142]

At the same time, Islam encourages debtors themselves not to procrastinate in repaying their debts. This is specially true in the case of wealthy debtors. The Prophet (saaw) said,

> *Procrastination (delay) in paying debts by a wealthy man is injustice.*[143]

If the businessman himself has incurred some debt in financing his business, he needs to repay them. In Islam, repayment of debts is so important that all the sins of a *shahīd* (martyr) are forgiven except for his unpaid debts.[144]

General Public. A businessman has a special obligation if he provides essential supplies to the public.[145] For example, the public has a need for farming produce, clothes, dwellings to inhabit. Since these are essential commodities, the businessman needs to price fairly. What steps can be taken if he is overcharging the public? Islam is against the idea of price con-

---

[141] *Qur'an* 2:280.
[142] Hudhayfah, *Ṣaḥīḥ al Bukhārī*, hadith no. 3.291.
[143] Abū Hurayrah, *Ṣaḥīḥ al Bukhārī*, hadith no. 3.486.
[144] Amr ibn al 'Āṣ, *Ṣaḥīḥ Muslim*, hadith no. 4649.
[145] Ibn Taymīyah, pp. 37-38 and Chapter 4.

trols.[146] The scholars who rule out price control altogether base themselves on the following hadith:

> *A man came and said, "Apostle of Allah, fix prices." He said, "(No), but I shall pray." Again the man came and said, "Apostle of Allah, fix prices." He said, "It is but Allah Who makes the prices low and high. I hope that when I meet Allah, none of you has any claim on me for doing wrong regarding blood or property."*[147]

Ibn Taymīyah points out, however, that this hadith does not discuss a situation where a merchant refuses to make a sale when under obligation to do so, or to perform an action legally required of him. Ibn Taymīyah concludes that should the businessman refuse to sell his goods at a fair price, he may be coerced by the imam to perform, and may also be punished for noncompliance.

Stockholders/Owners/Partners. Islam encourages partnerships. Any such project which aims at benefiting the individual or society or which removes some evil is righteous, especially if the intention of the investors is righteous a priori. Al Qaradāwī points out that such projects are blessed by Islam, and will receive Allah's help:

> *[...] Help you one another in righteousness and piety, but help you not one another in sin and rancor: [...]*[148]

- *Al Muḍārabah.* Frequently, the businessman may be a skillful entrepreneur, but lacks the venture capital to implement his business idea. In such cases, Islam allows partnering between capital and labor. This is called *al muḍārabah* or *al qirāḍ*. The venture capitalist or Islamic bank is considered as the owner of the capital invested whereas the entrepreneur contributes his or her expertise and skills. According to the Shari'ah, the two parties should agree in advance how they will share any profit or loss. Should the venture capitalist be guaranteed a profit on his capital whether his partner makes a profit or a loss, it would be similar to usury.[149] Further, no profits can be distributed until all losses have

[146] Loc. cit. and al Qaraḍāwī, p. 255.
[147] Abū Hurayrah, Abū Dāwūd, hadith no. 3443.
[148] *Qur'an* 5:2, and al Qaraḍāwī, p. 273.
[149] Al Qaraḍāwī, pp. 271-272.

been written off and the equity of the venture capitalist has been fully restored.[150]

- *Sharikat.*[151] There are several types of *sharikat* partnership. In one type of partnership, the Islamic bank provides part of the required capital while the businessman provides the balance. The businessman is also responsible for supervision and management. The two parties agree to share any profit or loss in proportion to their investment participation. Should there be a loss, it is considered sufficient if the businessman forfeits remuneration for his labor.
- *Mushārakah.* This type of partnership lasts a limited period of time, and endeavors to execute a specific project.[152] This resembles the Western joint venture or consortium. The parties agree to pitch in both fixed and working capital as well as expertise. They also agree how they will share any profits. Losses will be shared according to the proportion of committed capital.
- *Murābaḥah.* The bank purchases specific goods from the supplier on behalf of the entrepreneur for a fixed cost as well as an agreed upon profit margin. A key element of this type of financing is that both parties should know the initial purchase price as well as the profit markup. Second, the bank must acquire the goods before charging the entrepreneur. Once the merchandise is delivered, the two parties sign a sale contract on a cost-plus basis, and the entrepreneur takes possession of the goods. The businessman is to repay the bank the costs of goods sold as well as an agreed upon share of the profit according a predetermined schedule.
- *Qarḍ Ḥasan.* This arrangement is in the form of a "benevolent loan."[153] It does not include any charges, and is of course interest-free. This type of loan is made available to customers or businessmen experiencing hard times or incurring unexpected disbursements.

Whatever the form of partnership, the Islamic code of ethics requires all partners to be fair and to avoid cheating one another.

> *The Messenger of Allah (peace be upon him) having said, "Allah, Most High, says, 'I make a third with two partners as*

---

[150] Gani, p. 22.
[151] Gani, p. 18.
[152] Gambling and Karim, pp. 37-38.
[153] Loc. cit.

long as one of them does not cheat the other, but when he cheats him, I depart from them.'"[154]

The Needy. Very often, the needy will approach a businessman and ask for *ṣadaqah.* Sometimes, a businessman will give leftovers or spoiled goods that he would never consider using himself. For example, if a business person were to donate an old car that is in such poor condition that it endangers the life of anyone who attempts to drive it, then the donor is a wrong-doer. Allah warns us about this:

> *O you who believe! Give of the good things which you have (honorably) earned. And of the fruits of the earth which We have produced for you, and do not even aim at getting anything which is bad, in order that out of it you may give away something, when you yourselves would not receive it except with closed eyes.*[155]

Muslim businesses should give to the poor from what is wholesome and earned in a *ḥalāl* manner.

Competitors. Although the West claims to be for market competition, a cursory reading of key business publications will reveal that businesses are constantly seeking to assert themselves over and eliminate their competitors. By eliminating their competitors, firms can then reap above average economic returns through hoarding and monopolistic pricing. As per the discussion on hoarding on page 44, monopolies are discouraged in Islam.

> *It is abominable to monopolize*[156] *the necessaries of life, and food for cattle, in a city where such monopoly is likely to prove detrimental.*[157]

The Natural Environment

Another key domain of social responsibility is the natural environment. For many years, organizations got rid of their waste products by discharging

---

[154] Abū Hurayrah, Abū Dāwūd, hadith no. 3377.

[155] *Qur'an* 2:267.

[156] Arab, *Iḥtikār*. It is explained in the text to signify, in its literal sense, the laying up of anything; and in the language of the law, the purchasing of grain, or other necessaries of life, and keeping them up with a view to enhance the price.

[157] *Al Hidāyah* (Ḥanafi manual), vol. IV, 5857.

them in the air, into rivers and on land. Acid rain, global warming via depletion of the ozone layer, and poisoning of the food chain resulted from this irresponsible behavior. Nowadays, firms have realized the threat this practice poses to our natural environment, and are careful how they dispose of their waste. Firms such as Safeway use recycled paper in their paper bags, and McDonalds has changed the containers it now uses for packaging fast food.

Muslims are encouraged to appreciate the beauty of the natural environment. In fact, Allah refers to the beauty of the natural environment as one of His signs:

> *Seest thou not that Allah sends down rain from the sky? With it we then bring out produce of various colors. And in the mountains are tracts white and red, of various shades of color and black intense in hue. And so amongst men and crawling creatures and cattle are they of various colors. Those truly fear Allah, among His Servants who have knowledge.*[158]

Islam emphasizes man's role towards the natural environment by making him responsible of his surroundings as Allah's vicegerent.

> *Behold, thy Lord said to the angels, "I will create a vice-gerent on earth." They said, "Wilt thou place therein one who will make mischief therein and shed blood, whilst we do celebrate Thy praises and glorify Thy holy (name)?" He said, "I know what ye know not." And he taught Adam the names of all things: [...]*[159]

In his role as vicegerent, the Muslim businessman is expected to take care of his natural environment. The recent trend of *business environmentalism*, where businesses are being proactively very careful in the way they handle environmental concerns, is nothing new. Several instances exemplify the importance that Islam attaches to the natural environment: treatment of animals; environmental pollution and ownership rights; and environmental pollution of "free" natural resources such as air and water.

---

[158] *Qur'an* 35:27-28.

[159] *Qur'an* 2:30.

Treatment of Animals

Muslim businessmen who make use of animals must be extremely careful in how they treat them. Professional butchers, for example, must show kindness in slaughtering animals:

> *Two are the things which I remember Allah's Messenger (peace be upon him) having said, "Verily Allah has enjoined goodness to everything; so when you kill, kill in a good way and when you slaughter, slaughter in a good way. So every one of you should sharpen his knife, and let the slaughtered animal die comfortably."*[160]

While slaughtering an animal, Muslims are also discouraged from seizing an animal destined for slaughter by the feet, and dragging it to the place where it will be slaughtered.[161]

Farmers, too, need to be careful. Even in our daily treatment of animals, the Prophet (saaw) has encouraged Muslims to show consideration towards them:

> *Allah's Messenger (peace be upon him) said, "A prostitute was forgiven by Allah, because, passing by a panting dog near a well and seeing that the dog was about to die of thirst, she took off her shoe, and tying it with her head-cover she drew out some water for it. So, Allah forgave her because of that."*[162]

Certain types of behavior have been explicitly forbidden:

> *Allah's Messenger (peace be upon him) forbade (the animals to be beaten) on the face or cauterization on the face.*[163]

Additionally, Muslims are discouraged from inciting animals to fight with one another. As a result, Muslims should not engage in businesses involving pitbull or other animal fights.

---

[160] Shaddād ibn 'Aws, *Ṣaḥīḥ Muslim*, hadith no. 4810.

[161] *Al Hidāyah* (Ḥanafi manual), vol. 4, 5764.

[162] Abū Hurayrah, *Ṣaḥīḥ al Bukhārī*, hadith no. 4.538.

[163] Jābir ibn 'Abd Allāh, *Ṣaḥīḥ Muslim*, hadith no. 5281.

Environmental Pollution and Ownership Rights

Although Islam honors ownership rights, it does not consider these rights to be absolute especially if they may lead to environmental pollution and threaten public safety. For example, Muslims are also prevented from slaughtering animals in the streets or houses in order to avoid unsanitary conditions.[164] Similarly, to reduce the danger of public safety and environmental hazards, Muslims were not allowed to install a forge, a threshing floor, a cook shop or a mill in residential areas.[165]

Once a Muslims pollutes the environment, he is expected to clean it up or remove what is causing the pollution:

> *If any person constructs a cesspit or a sewer near a well of water belonging to some other person, and contaminates the water thereof, he may be made to remove the injury. If it is impossible to remove the injury, he may be made to close up the cesspit or sewer. Again, if any person constructs a sewer near to a water channel, and the dirty water from such sewer flows into the channel and causes great injury thereto, and no other way can be found to remove such injury than by closing it, the sewer shall be closed.*[166]

Conversely, businesses cannot be held responsible for noise or other types of environmental problems under certain conditions. Thus, if a business is already set up in a location, and an individual builds a house next to it, the owner of the new house cannot complain about noise, dust or other sources of disturbance resulting from his proximity to the business:

> *If any person deals with property owned in absolute ownership in some manner authorized by law, and some other person constructs a building by the side thereof whereby he suffers injury, he himself alone must remove such injury.*[167]

Under this specific circumstance, the business cannot be compelled to stop the noise or control the dust, or even to close down.

---

[164] Khan, M. Akram. 1992. "Al Ḥisbah and the Islamic Economy" In Ibn Taymīyah's *Public Duties in Islam: The Institution of the Ḥisbah*, p. 145.

[165] *Al Majallah* (The Ottoman Courts Manual [Ḥanafī]), serial no. 2432, paragraph 1200.

[166] Ibid., serial no. 2444, paragraph 1212.

[167] Ibid., serial no. 2439, paragraph 1207.

Environmental Pollution and Free Resources (air, water, etc.)

The general principle with respect to resources that are free, e.g., air, ocean water, etc. is the following:

> *Any person may make use of any thing that is free provided that is doing so no injury is inflicted upon any other person.*[168]

Should injury or pollution of any kind take place, the guilty party must then be responsible either of cleaning after himself or of removing the cause of the problem:

> *Any person may water his lands from rivers which are not owned in absolute ownership by any particular person, and, in order to irrigate them and to construct mills, may open a canal or water channels, provided that he does not thereby inflict injury on any other person. Consequently, if the water overflows and causes injury to the public, or the water of the river is entirely cut off, or boats cannot be navigated, such injury must be stopped.*[169]

The General Social Welfare

Besides behaving responsibly towards their stakeholders and the natural environment, Muslims and the organizations they work in are expected to care about the general welfare of the society they live in. As part of the community, Muslim businessmen need to watch over the welfare of its weak and destitute members.

> *And why should you not fight in the cause of Allah and of those who, being weak, are ill treated (and oppressed)?—men, women and children, [...]*[170]

The reward for taking care of the destitute and the weak is stressed in this hadith:

> *The Prophet (peace be upon him) said, "The one who looks after and works for a widow and for a poor person, is like a*

---

[168] Ibid., serial no. 2486, paragraph 1254.
[169] Ibid., serial no. 2497, paragraph 1265.
[170] *Qur'an* 4:75.

warrior fighting for Allah's cause or like a person who fasts during the day and prays all the night."[171]

On the other hand, if any person spends the night hungry, the blame is shared by the community because it did not attempt to take care of him.[172]

Muslim businesses contribute to charities, and support many philanthropic causes. For example, Amana, a Muslim investment company, sponsored and published a revised edition of the translation of the Holy Qur'an by Yūsuf 'Alī. Similarly, the Association of Muslim Scientists and Engineers published a guide to answer the questions of foreign Muslim students seeking admission to North American universities. The Red Crescent is an internationally known organizations, operating in Muslim countries to provide relief to the poor and destitute during times of crisis.

Arguments For and Against Social Responsibility

The issue of the social responsibility of business is a much debated one. Table 5 summarizes the arguments that have been advanced both for and against this issue. Stakeholders in favor of social responsibility argue that since businesses are the source of problems such as pollution, they need to fix them. The counterargument is that businesses, by making a profit and sharing it with society in the form of wages and taxes, have already paid their share, and should not be held accountable for problems that may not be completely avoidable.

Those in favor of social responsibility suggest that to the extent that businesses understand the nature of the problems they have created, they are better equipped to solve them. Unlike governments which are financially strapped, businesses can set aside a portion of their resources and profits to clean up after themselves. Advocates against social responsibility decry the enormous power of corporations once they have adopted a social cause. Because of the magnitude of their financial contributions, corporations can derail social causes, transforming them into advertising gimmicks serving to enhance their profits.

Getting involved in social causes accumulates goodwill towards the company. McDonalds' sponsorship of children in need of help through the Ronald McDonalds program enhances the corporation's image as a good citizen who cares. Alternately, many businesses do not know how to run

---

171 Safwān ibn Salīm, *Ṣaḥīḥ al Bukhārī*, 8.35.

172 Kotb, Sayed. *Social Justice in Islam*. New York: Octagon, 1970. p. 65. Also in As Sayyid Sābiq. *Fiqh-us-Sunna*, 3. 93c, Paragraph 10.

such a program. A business which manufactures biological weapons may have a rough time either in managing a social program such as the March of Dimes, or may not be welcome by the public.

Finally, in contrast to secular law, Islam may not recognize the existence of a business as a corporate legal entity whose owners are not personally accountable for the problems created by it. Hence, if a business creates a problem, then its owners are liable for cleaning up. If they do not clean up, they may actually be forced to do so:

> *Should all the owners of a right of taking water refuse to clean a river which is jointly owned, they may be forced to do so, if it is a public river, but not if it is a private river.*[173]

Organizational Modes of Social Responsiveness

In responding to demands for greater social responsibility, an organization can be responsive in four ways: social obstruction, social obligation, social response and social contribution. These can be arrayed along a continuum extending from low to high social responsiveness, and are not discrete categories within which an organization can be fitted.[174]

Social Obstruction. Firms in this category are the least socially responsive. They try to avoid their social responsibilities, or do as little as possible when dealing with problems of their own making. For example, in a small city in Nevada, petroleum companies whose holding tanks have been leaking into underground water have tried to deny responsibility, and are taking the city council to court in order to deny guilt. Similarly, Intel refused to provide all owners of defective Pentium computers with a replacement chip until public outbursts compelled it to.

Social Obligation. Organizations do the bare minimum required under the law, but nothing more. For example, automobile manufacturers place seat belts and exhaust filters in their cars because they are required to. They do not provide additional safety mechanisms because it would increase their costs and reduce their profit margin.

---

[173] *Al Majallah,* Serial No 2556, Reference, *Al Majallah* (The Ottoman Courts Manual [Hanafi]), 1324.

[174] Barney and Griffin, pp. 734-735.

Table 5[175]
Arguments For and Against Social Responsibility

Arguments for Social Responsibility	Arguments Against Social Responsibility
Business creates problems and are responsible for solving them.	The purpose of business is profit maximization. By paying taxes and wages, they have done their share.
Business has the resources needed to solve problems.	Conflicts of interest may arise since charitable causes may become marketing tools for corporations.
Social responsibility enhances goodwill towards the organization.	Business may not know how to manage social programs.
Islam does not neccssarily recognize businesses as legal entities whose obligations are separate from its owners.[176]	Corporations are merely legal entities, and cannot be held personally liable for problems they cause.

Social Response. Firms with a social response strategy observe their legal requirements, and exceed these requirements wherever possible. For example, IBM also gives surplus computers to schools. Other businesses work hard both at hiring minorities, and providing them with minority scholarships at various universities.

Social Contribution. Firms in this category are the most socially responsive. They embrace the demands of their social role, and actively seek out opportunities to help. Hewlett Packard not only asks users of toner for their laser printers to send back the potentially polluting toner cartridges, but will also pay for these cartridges to be sent back.

Managing Social Responsibility

Organizations must be proactive with respect to concerns involving social responsibility. Just as they mastermind strategic thrusts to develop competitive advantage in the marketplace, they need to use a number of

---

[175] Barney, Jay B. & Griffin, Ricky W. *The Management of Organizations.* © 1992 by Houghton Mifflin Company, pp. 732-734. Adapted with permission.

[176] Whether a firm can or cannot be a legal entity according to Islam is still being debated. See Gambling and Karim, pp. 36-37.

tools to enhance their social responsiveness. Some of these tools can be explicitly stated whereas others are more implicit.

Explicit Organizational Approaches

Developing a Code of Ethics

By developing a code of ethics with the participation of their employees, organizations are sending a signal to their stakeholders about their ethical intent. By training their employees in ethics and rewarding them for ethical behavior, they are encouraging organizational participants to behave ethically. Table 6 illustrates how Honeywell stresses certain key values through its code of ethics.

Table 6
Honeywell's Three R's[177]

- ♦ *Under our ethical behavior model, every employee has the following responsibilities:*
  - *recognize an issue or situation*
  - *raise the issue or situation to the appropriate levels*
  - *see them through to resolution*
- ♦ *The company has the responsibility to create and clearly communicate policies and procedures so that employees know what is expected of them.*
- ♦ *We preach the concept of self-governance.*

In developing a code of ethics, Muslim managers should:[178]

1. Identify the key stakeholders of the company, and the organization's responsibility to each in accordance to the Islamic moral code. The list of stakeholders that Muslim businesses may wish to consider are discussed in the section on stakeholders.
2. Define ethical values or draw up specific behavioral guidelines for each of the stakeholders the company interacts with. The abovementioned section on stakeholders surveys the Islamic ethical concepts that affect the company's stakeholders (Keeping promises, honesty, respect for people, benevolence, justice, etc.). Table 7 presents a sample code of ethics for Muslim businesses.

---

[177] Honeywell Corporation.

[178] Modified from material presented in (1) Luthans, F., Hodgetts, R. M. and Thompson, K. R. 1990. *Social Issues in Business: Strategic and Public Policy Perspectives*. New York: Macmillan, pp. 120-128, and (2) Collins, D. and O'Rourke, T. 1994. *Ethical Dilemmas in Business*. Cincinnati, OH: pp. 52-53.

3. Investigate what other ethical codes influence employees' behavior in the organization, and if possible, design the corporate code so as not to clash with these external codes of conduct.[179]
4. Describe how the company actually deals with its stakeholders, and focus on areas where there may be a gap between the Islamic code of conduct and the *actual* behavior of the company.
5. Determine how to narrow the gap uncovered in step 3.
6. Form a system of internal controls in order to track specific practices.
7. Formulate a management policy for responding to unethical behavior and for encouraging ethical conduct.
8. Annually evaluate the code. What gaps still exist? What new ethical issues have emerged?
9. Adjust the code or its implementation. Although the Islamic code of behavior as outlined in the Qur'an and the Sunnah may not be modified, there may be alternate ways to encourage employees (including management) to behave ethically.

In implementing develop a code of ethics, several mechanisms are need to ensure its success:

- Managers must be involved during the whole process. They can guide employees towards ethical behavior by acting as role models. Using the earlier principles that al Qaraḍāwī developed to distinguish *ḥalāl* from *ḥarām* behavior, Muslim managers can clarify that rationalizations for unethical behavior are unacceptable. Should some executives pad their expense account because everybody else does it, the managers must send a clear message that such behavior will not be tolerated.[180]
- New recruits must learn about the organization's ethical standards before they join. This step will deter potentially unethical employees from coming on board.
- Established employees need training in ethics. By knowing what the standards are, they will be less upset when they are censured for any unethical action.
- Provide alternate ways for employees to report potential violation of the code of ethics by peers, subordinates or superiors.

---

[179] Weiss, p. 269.

[180] Bhide, A. and Stevenson, H. H. "Why Be Honest if Honesty Doesn't Pay?" *Harvard Business Review*, September-October 1990, 121-129.

- Any report of an ethical problem should be followed by a fair, prompt and objective hearing.[181]
- Whistle blowing to an organization ombudsperson outside the chain of command will not be cause for retaliation.
- Top management support of the code of ethics should be demonstrated through strict enforcement against those who behave unethically.

Ethical Oversight

By appointing key organizational actors to a ethics review panel, and by having its actions reviewed by this panel, an organization will ensure compliance both with legal regulations and the ethical concerns of all key stakeholders.

Table 7
Sample Code of Ethics for Muslim Businesses

Insha Allah, we will behave Islamically towards:

- ***Our Customers:***
  Our primary responsibility is to provide the best quality product to those who make use of our products and services. We must work to decrease our costs in order to charge reasonable prices. Orders will be processed speedily and without errors. We will neither misrepresent nor deny our products or services to any customer on the basis of race, religion or national origin.

- ***Our Suppliers and Distributors:***
  We will work with our suppliers and distributors to maintain consistency in quality and service. We will ensure that they make a fair profit. We shall neither offer nor accept any premium, prize or other un-Islamic inducement in our transactions with our suppliers and distributors, or any other stakeholder.

- ***Our Employees:***
  Every employee will work in safe and clean conditions. They will receive fair and adequate compensation. They will have ample opportunities to develop their skills. They must feel free to make suggestions, criticize or complain. We will safeguard their rights to privacy, protect them from any type of harassment and respect their dignity at all times. The company will clearly communicate to all employees what is expected of them. In all negotiations,

[181] Weiss, pp. 268-269.

we will act in good faith. Every employee shall take responsibility to ensure that their actions are in agreement with Islamic values and the Code of ethics of this company.

- ***Our Competitors:***
  We will not engage in monopolistic behavior and preclude others from competing with us. We will compete fairly without engaging in un-Islamic tactics.

- ***Our Stockholders:***
  We must work to ensure a fair return to our stockholders. We will only engage in what is halal and stay away from the haram. We will manage our research and development projects wisely. We will compensate our employees equitably. We will maintain appropriate reserves for difficult times. We will not waste company resources on false needs. When we behave according to our code of ethics, we should be able to provide our stockholders with an Islamically acceptable rate of return.

- ***Our Community:***
  We support the community we live in as well as the world ummah. We will be good citizens, paying our fair share of taxes and contributing to the welfare of the needy and the destitute. We will protect our environment and natural resources.

Appointment of an Ethics Advocate

This person can probe management's decisions regularly, checking into the rationale and purpose that underlie them. For an ethics advocate to fulfill his or her role effectively, management may not restrict the type of decisions that are called into question. Although a subordinate is often appointed to this role, the ethics of macro and strategic level decisions can better be explored by an advocate with adequate organizational experience, but outstanding moral credibility.

Selection and Training

By training new recruits in the code of ethics, and providing a realistic job preview where they learn about the firm's ethical behavior, those who join the firm will do so with a clear understanding of the ethical component of their job. They will also be more likely to behave ethically without the fear of downward pressure or the threat of losing their jobs.

Adjusting the Reward System

The law of effect[182] suggests that behavior which is rewarded will be repeated. Behavior which is not rewarded will not be repeated. An organization which explicitly rewards Islamic behavior will encourage the re-occurrence of such behavior. Alternately, an organization which lets unethical behavior go unpunished will find itself in trouble sooner or later. The example of the Muslim banking firm BCCI filing for bankruptcy after it tolerated business improprieties should be kept in mind.

Implicit Organizational Approaches

Changing the Culture. An Islamic organization has a built-in set of values. These values stem from the Qur'an and Sunnah, and are incorporated with the Islamic Code of Ethics outlined earlier. Unfortunately, many Islamic organizations feel compelled to adopt alien, un-Islamic values when they come into contact with secular, global corporations. Adjusting an organization's culture is traumatic and lengthy, depending upon which level of culture the organizational leaders wish to change. At the surface level, artifacts such as symbols reflecting the ethical position of the organization are relatively easy to changed. Deeper aspects of culture, such as the core beliefs and values of organizational participants will require consistent emphasis on an agreed upon set of ethical beliefs and values. Exemplary ethical behavior by the organizational leader will also be needed to steer his or her subordinates towards the desired types of behavior. Thus, the advent of Islam changed the pan-Arabic culture from one based on tribal loyalties and *jāhilīyah* to one based on the command of Allah and the exemplary model of the Prophet (saw). Having been duly trained in the ethical code of Islam, the envoys of the Islamic state to distant lands such as Persia and Byzantium did not have to wait for a decision from the Caliph: they already knew what to do under different and often adverse circumstances.

Whistle-blowing. Whistle-blowing is an employee's reporting of unethical conduct by other co-workers. The term "whistle-blower" is used to refer to people who disclose wrong-doing for moral reasons.[183] Whistle-blowing is an important process whereby the organization can obtain information about activities that threaten the moral fiber of the organization. Whistle-blowers have traditionally had to risk their career or hostile reper-

---

[182] Thorndike.

[183] James, Gene. 1990. "Whistle-blowing: Its Moral Justification." In P. Marsden and J. Shafritz, *Essentials of Business Ethics*. New York: Penguin, pp. 162-190.

cussions in order to get their message heard. Organizations need to develop an informal channel of communication whereby the whistle-blower can report the incident without any fear of a backlash. At times, the whistle-blower may have to go to an outside regulatory agency or to the media to report questionable organizational behavior.

Performing a Social Audit

A *corporate social audit* seeks to determine how effective an organization's social performance is.[184] To pass such an audit, the organization must clearly state its social objectives, determine whether it has the resources to meet each objective, assess how these objectives are being met, and suggest which areas need further improvement.

Two approaches developed to assess how corporations are responding to employee and community needs are: the General Electric approach and the First Bank Minneapolis approach. The General Electric approach helps the firm to (a) define both corporate and component goals and objectives, (b) explore how the company is using its resources, (c) trace out the consequences of managerial actions, and (d) distinguish among various courses of action. The First Bank Minneapolis approach identifies key constituents to which the firm feels responsible: public safety, income, health, transportation, etc. A firm following the bank approach will then set objectives for itself in each of these areas, and begin measuring its performance. The firm may simultaneously develop a Community Quality of Life Report, assessing trends in quality of life indicators such as education, housing, jobs, etc. in its market area. The results of the Bank approach indicate the bank's progress in meeting its community responsibilities and help to track which public priorities are being met. Table 8 describes the steps that may be undertaken during a social audit.

---

[184] Hellriegel, D. and Slocum, J. *Management*, Reading, MA: Addison-Wesley Publishing Co., 1992, p. 169.

Table 8[185]
The Social Audit Process

Steps	Contents
Determine social expectations	Investigate what key stakeholders expect from the company and within what areas.
Outline firm's position and response	Determine where the firm stands with respect to various stakeholder demands, and explain how the firm will respond to these.
State program objectives and resources committed.	Break down response to stakeholder demands into program areas, and outline objectives for each program area. For example, cut down by 50% pollution produced by smokestacks through the use of special equipment.
Monitor progress and implement corrections	Assess the degree to which program objectives are being met, and make necessary corrections.

General Ethical Guidelines for Muslims in Business

Some general guidelines govern the Islamic code of ethics with relation to both one's daily life and business conduct. Muslims are required to behave Islamically in their business dealings because Allah Himself is witness to their transactions:

> *In whatever business you may be, and whatever portion you may be reciting from the Qur'an—and whatever deed you (mankind) may be doing—We are Witnesses thereof when you are deeply engrossed therein. [...]*[186]

Here are some key business principles that Muslims should follow.

Be Honest and Truthful. Honesty and truthfulness are qualities which a Muslim businessman should develop and practice in himself. Truth, for example, has a self-reinforcing effect. In a hadith reported in *Ṣaḥīḥ al Bukhārī*,

---

[185] Loc. cit.
[186] *Qur'an* 10:61.

> *The Prophet (peace be upon him) said, "Truthfulness leads to righteousness, and righteousness leads to Paradise. A man continued to tell the truth until he becomes a truthful person. Falsehood leads to al fujūr (i.e., wickedness, evil-doing), and al fujūr (wickedness) leads to the (Hell) Fire, and a man may continue to tell lies till he is written before Allah, a liar."*[187]

Honesty and truth is especially important for Muslim business persons because of the need to make a profit and the temptations to enhance the attributes of their product or service during a sales pitch. This is why the Prophet (saaw) said:

> *The merchants will be raised on the Day of Resurrection as evil-doers, except those who fear Allah, are honest and speak the truth.*[188]

Keep Your Word. In a hadith narrated by Abū Hurayrah, the Prophet (saaw) is reported to have said:

> *The Prophet (peace be upon him) said, "If you guarantee me six things on your part I shall guarantee you Paradise. Speak the truth when you talk, keep a promise when you make it, when you are trusted with something fulfill your trust, avoid sexual immorality, lower your eyes, and restrain your hands from injustice."*[189]

Love Allah More Than Your Trade. We must love Allah even if we have to sacrifice everything else. Allah warns in the Qur'an,

> *Say, "If it be that your fathers, your sons, your brothers, your mates, or your kindred; the wealth that you have gained; the commerce in which you fear a decline; or the dwellings in which you delight—are dearer to you than Allah, or His Messenger, or the striving in His cause—then*

---

[187] 'Abd Allāh, in *Ṣaḥīḥ al Bukhārī*, hadith no. 8.116.

[188] Tirmidhī, Ibn Mājah and Dārimī transmitted it, and Bayhaqī transmitted it in *Shu'ab al Īmān* on the authority of al Barā'. *Mishkāt al Maṣābīḥ*, 2799.

[189] 'Ubādah ibn al Ṣāmit, Aḥmad and Bayhaqī transmitted it, *Mishkāt al Maṣābīḥ*, 4870.

wait until Allah brings about His Decision: and Allah guides not the rebellious."[190]

Deal with Muslims before Dealing with Non-Muslims. In a sound hadith, the Prophet (saaw) hired a polytheist as a guide at the time of his migration from Makkah to Madinah, thus entrusting him with his life and money. The people of the tribe of Khuzā'ah, who included both Muslims and non-Muslims, acted as scouts for the Prophet (saaw). In a hadith reported by Sa'd, the Prophet (saaw) asked Muslims to seek medical treatment from al Ḥārith ibn Kaldah, who was a disbeliever.[191] However, as As Sayyid Ṣābiq pointed out, if a Muslim physician is present, one should seek his or her treatment and not turn to anyone else. The same applies when one has to entrust a person with funds or deal with him in business.[192]

Be Humble in how You Conduct Your Life. Muslims must not lead a life of extravagance, and must exhibit good-will in any transactions among themselves.

> *O you who believe! Eat not up your property among yourselves in vanities: but let there be amongst you traffic and trade by mutual good-will: nor kill (or destroy) yourselves: for verily Allah has been to you Most Merciful.*[193]

Use Mutual Consultation in Your Affairs. In describing the characteristics of those who will receive higher and more permanent gifts from Him, Allah stresses the importance of consultation.

> *Those who hearken to their Lord; and establish regular prayer; who (conduct) their affairs by mutual consultation, who spend out of what we bestow on them for sustenance.*[194]

Do Not Deal in Fraud. Businessmen should avoid duplicity. They should treat others in the same righteous and fair manner that they themselves would like to be treated.

---

[190] *Qur'an* 9:24.
[191] Abū Dāwūd, hadith no. 3866.
[192] *Fiqh-us-Sunnah,* 4, 6.a, paragraph 4.
[193] *Qur'an* 4:29.
[194] *Qur'an* 42:38.

Woe to those that deal in fraud those who when they have to receive by measure from men exact full measure. But when they have to give by measure or weight to men give less than due. Do they not think that they will be called to account?[195]

Do Not Bribe. Businessmen may sometimes be tempted to offer bribes or *baqshīsh* in order to persuade another party to give them special favors or to allow them to get away with dishonest practices. The practice of bribery is forbidden in Islam.

The Apostle of Allah (peace be upon him) cursed the one who bribes and the one who takes bribes.[196]

Deal Justly. The general principle that applies across all transactions including those pertaining to businesses is that of justice or *'adl.* Allah emphasizes this point in the Qur'an:

Deal not unjustly, and you shall not be dealt with unjustly.[197]

In applying the above guidelines, Muslims may wish to use the checklist in Table 9 to examine the ethics of a business decision. The questions in this checklist[198] draw from the ethical philosophy of Islam, but avoid the level of abstraction typically connected with moral reasoning.

Punishment and Repentance for Unethical Behavior

No Coercion in Ethical Behavior

Just as there is no compulsion in religion, one cannot generate goodness in one's business peers by coercion. Muslims have to choose to be ethical. This is why Allah has given us free will. Born in a state of *fiṭrah*, we later choose our *dīn*. If an individual misbehaves after reaching the age of reason, we should investigate why he did so before inflicting any penalty (*ḥudd*). He may have behaved unethically either because of extenuating circumstances

---

[195] *Qur'an* 83:1-4.

[196] 'Abd Allāh ibn 'Amr ibn al 'Āṣ, Abū Dāwūd, hadith no. 3573.

[197] *Qur'an* 2:279.

[198] Adapted from Nash, Laura. "Ethics without the Sermon." In Peter Marsden and Jay Shafritz (eds.), *Essentials of Business Ethics.* New York: Penguin, pp. 38-61.

circumstances, he may not be punished. The Prophet (saaw) emphasized the importance of delaying and interceding before inflicting punishment.

If you make intercession, you will be rewarded.[199]

Table 9

A Checklist for Assessing the Ethical Nature of a Business Decision[a]

1. Have you defined the problem accurately?
2. How would you define the problem if you stood on the other side of the fence?
3. How did this situation occur in the first place?
4. To whom and to what do you give your loyalty as an individual and a member of this organization?
5. What is your intention or *niyyat* in making this decision?
6. How does this intention compare with the probable results?
7. Whom does your decision or action help or injure?
8. Can you discuss the problem with the affected parties before you make your decision?
9. Are you confident that your position will be as valid over a long period of time as it seems now?
10. Could you disclose without qualm your decision or action to your boss, the board of directors, your peers, your subordinates, your family, society as a whole?
11. What is the symbolic potential of your action if understood? If misunderstood?
12. Under what conditions would you allow exceptions to your stand?

[a]Reprinted by permission of *Harvard Business Review*. Exhibit From "Ethics without the Sermon," by Laura L. Nash, Nov-Dec 1981. Copyright © 1981 by the President and Fellows of Harvard College, all rights reserved.

Should an investigation of the circumstances surrounding unethical behavior indicate that a person is responsible for some wrongdoing, society cannot be criticized for inflicting an appropriate penalty on him. However,

[199] Mu'āwiyah, Abū Dāwūd, 5113.

the penalty is not so much punishment for punishment's sake. In Islamic ethics, the penalty administered by society is more for reforming the guilty party, and safeguarding society at large from the impact of his mischief. If the Muslim who is punished for unethical behavior repents and amends his behavior, he is not to be harassed for his previous behavior. He should not be cast away for two reasons. First, Allah is the one who grants forgiveness and mercy. He states in the Qur'an,

> *But if the thief repents after his crime, and amends his conduct, Allah turns to him in forgiveness; for Allah is Oft-Forgiving, Most Merciful.*[200]

Second, once the unethical Muslim repents, he is part of the ummah again.

> *'Ikrimah narrated from ibn 'Abbās that he said that Allah's Messenger (peace be upon him) said, "When a slave (of Allah) commits illegal sexual intercourse, he is not a believer at the time of committing it; and if he steals he is not a believer at the time of stealing; and if he drinks alcohol, then he is not a believer at the time of drinking it; and he is not a believer when he commits a murder."*

> *'Ikrimah said, "I asked ibn 'Abbās, 'How is faith taken away from him?' He said, 'Like this,' clasping his hands and then separating them, and added, 'but if he repents, faith returns to him like this,' clasping his hands again."*[201]

Punishment Philosophy in Islam

Once faith returns to the unethical person, abusing him is sinful.

> *The Prophet (peace be upon him) said, "Abusing a Muslim is* fusūq *(an evil deed) and killing him is* kufr *(unbelief)."*[202]

---

[200] *Qur'an* 5:39.
[201] 'Abd Allāh ibn 'Abbās, *Ṣaḥīḥ al Bukhārī*, 8.800B.
[202] 'Abd Allāh ibn Mas'ūd, *Ṣaḥīḥ al Bukhārī*, 1.46.

In general, then, the duty of a Muslim is to behave ethically. Should he err, he should receive the punishment he deserves unless there are extenuating circumstances. Once he has been punished, he is one of the ummah again if he repents. Thereafter, he should not be persecuted for his previous wrongs.

Experiential Exercises and Questionnaires

Recep Saleh's Ethical Dilemma [203]

In 1990, an important ethical question came up at the July Board of Directors' meeting at Saleh Pipe Building, Inc. At the time, the family-owned producer of pipes and other oil refinery specialty equipment had annual sales of $300 million. According to Recep Saleh, the company's Chief Executive Officer, this is what happened during the meeting.

"As the July meeting began, I was feeling rather happy with myself. The audited results for 1990 were far better than had been forecasted. Although Turkey was in the middle of a worldwide recession, our firm had performed surprisingly well during the first two quarters of 1990. I was not too worried about the state of the Turkish economy because of some potentially lucrative overseas projects.

Several years earlier, the board had encouraged our top managers to expand into foreign markets. Since then, we had built and serviced refineries in Mexico and Malaysia. The promising ventures that I was looking forward to would take place in a Third World country which, for reasons that will soon be apparent, cannot be named. I had taken several trips to that country and reached an agreement under which we would supply the equipment and training to enable a domestic oil refinery to grow and strengthen its operations. In return, we would be given a substantial equity position in the company. The best part of the deal was that our firm would not have to put up any cash.

There was, however, one problem with this project. The manager of the oil refinery had openly admitted to me that they were paying off the government of their country in order to do business. I knew that several board members would not agree to do business with this company; yet, I did not anticipate strong objections given the depressed condition of the global economy. The ethical practices of the foreign company seemed to be as irrelevant as they would be if they were just buying equipment from us. Further, although the laws of this third world country prohibit bribery, it is common practice there.

After introducing the proposal at the meeting, I briefly mentioned the payoff complication. I then asked for a motion for approval to place the proposal formally before the board. The motion was made and seconded. Everything was moving smoothly when suddenly Abdallah Cengel (a lawyer and

[203] This case was constructed from material published in *Fortune*, 1976.

my friend from my *madrasah* days) stood up and started highlighting the ethical problems associated with dealing with a company that was bribing its government. I didn't see why our own company would become unethical just by owning stock in an unethical company. Initially, I did not realize that Abdallah was going to oppose the deal. Then some other board members began to voice similar concerns. One of the board members then suggested setting up a new sales company to handle the payoffs, leaving us free to participate in the project with the foreign company. Many board members opposed this suggestion, which would just be covering up the issue.

Abdallah was objecting to the project relentlessly, saying, "I don't care whether there is any legal exposure or not. We are Muslims working for a Muslim company; we are responsible to a Higher Authority! I don't want Saleh Pipe Building, Inc. to participate in a company that's paying off its government, and that's that." Angry, I fired off the following remark, "Don't you realize that if we adopt this policy, we'll be shut out of half the world? Don't you realize that our competition in Europe, Japan and Korea won't have any such ethical qualms and will shut us out of this market permanently? What has happened to our policy of international expansion? Do you want our company to go bankrupt? Without access to global markets, we cannot survive!"

An Ethics Test

Many situations in day-to-day business are not simple right-or-wrong questions, but rather fall into a gray area. To demonstrate the perplexing array of moral dilemmas faced by Muslims, here is a "nonscientific" test for slippage ... Don't expect to score high. That is not the purpose, But give it a try, and see how you do. Please, put your value system to the test in the following situations:

Scoring Card: **SA** = Strongly agree **A** = Agree
DA = Disagree **SA** = Strongly Disagree

		SA	A	D	SD
1.	Employees should not be expected to inform on their peers for wrong doings.	___	___	___	___
2.	There are times when a manager must overlook contract and safety violations in order to get on with the job.	___	___	___	___
3.	It is not always possible to keep accurate expense account records; therefore, it is sometimes necessary to give approximate figures.	___	___	___	___
4.	There are times when it is necessary to withhold embarrassing information from one's superior.	___	___	___	___
5.	We should do what our managers suggest, though we may have doubts about its being the right thing to do.	___	___	___	___
6.	It is sometimes necessary to conduct personal business on company time.	___	___	___	___
7.	Sometimes, it is good psychology to set goals above normal if it will help to obtain a greater effort from the sales force.	___	___	___	___
8.	I would quote a 'hopeful' shipping date in order to get the order.	___	___	___	___
9.	It is proper to use the company long distance telephone line for personal calls as long as it's not for a long call.	___	___	___	___
10.	Management must be goal-oriented; therefore, the end usually justifies the means.	___	___	___	___

11.	If it takes entertainment and twisting company policy to win a large contract, I would authorize it.	___	___	___	___
12.	Exceptions to company policy and procedures are a way of life.	___	___	___	___
13.	If a customer overpays his account, it is O.K. However, if he underpays his account, we must investigate the matter at once.	___	___	___	___
14.	Occasional use of the company's photocopier for personal or community activities is acceptable.	___	___	___	___
15.	Taking home company property (pencils, paper, tape, etc.) for personal use is an accepted fringe benefit.	___	___	___	___

Scoring key:

Strongly Disagree	=	0
Disagree	=	1
Agree	=	2
Strongly Agree	=	3

If your score is 0, you have very strong ethical values.
If your score is 1-5, you have relatively strong ethical values.
If your score is 6-10, you have somewhat strong ethical values.
If your score is 11-15, you have good ethical values.
If your score is 16-25, you have average ethical values.
If your score is 26-35, you need to improve your code of ethics.
If your score is 36 or above, you are slipping fast, and need help re-establishing a code of ethics.

The above instrument has been adapted with permission from Lowell G. Rein's "Is Your (Ethical) Slippage Showing?," *Personnel Journal*, September 1986, © 1986.

Oil And Gas Exploration (Malaysia) Ltd.[204]

Cary Reed smoked pensively in his luxurious office on the fourteenth floor of the OGEL tower in downtown Penang. A gorgeous sunset illuminated the sea and cheered him up after the humid heat of the day. As Managing Director of OGEL responsible for Malaysia, he was writing his quarterly report to George Dahl, the VP of the international division located at OGEL's home office in New York City.

"The Anwar Ahmad problem is very complex. I have never faced a problem like this before. My other overseas assignment in Germany was so smooth compared to what I have to deal with here. Over there, in Germany, they respected the authority of OGEL managers. Whenever I asked them to do something, they rushed to do it—no questions asked. Even when I requested them to work through Sunday, they did not object as long they got their overtime pay. Here, I am not sure whether Anwar Ahmad or the Malay culture is the obstacle.

One of the tasks that I have been assigned here is to locate and train Malays with high potential for top management positions. Anwar Ahmad is one of hottest trainees. He has proven himself in his past assignments as an on-site supervisor and more recently as an area assistant manager. He was sent to the Executive Management Program at Stanford University, and came through successfully. As a result, I had him and several other promising Malays on a fast track to become regional managers for OGEL within the next five years.

What I overlooked was that these Malay trainees are all Muslims. As you may be aware, Islamic zeal is becoming more intense in Malaysia. This may be partly because of the rise of Islam internationally. Ever since Iran deposed the Shah, Muslim countries have not been the same. Here, the movement towards Islam is obstructing the Malayanization program of this country's government.

OGEL wants its managers to believe in its corporate culture in order to ensure consistency of behavior across its overseas divisions. The Malay trainees we have selected do not fit the typical OGEL managerial profile. In fact, my previous discussions with Anwar's boss revealed that he (Anwar) is currently non promotable without further training in finance, communication and personnel. Why? He has refused assignments meant to develop his managerial skills. For example, I recently wanted to place him in charge of a

---

[204] This case has been modified with permission from the *Transcontinental Industries (Malaysia) Ltd. case* in Hellriegel and Slocum, p. 142. © 1992 by Hellriegel and Slocum.

new oil exploration venture. He refused the job because one of his tasks would involve seeking financing from banks, and such financing involved interest. What am I to do? If Anwar and the other Malay trainees do not advance up the corporate ladder, they could complain to the governmental authorities. Our chances of bidding on future exploration ventures either on or off-shore would be damaged.

If I were to pinpoint the source of the problem, I would say that Anwar is too eager about Islam to be a successful OGEL executive. Some of the Imams have recently stated on local TV and in the local press that Islamic nations should be guard against westernizing their culture and economy. My encounters with Anwar have confirmed that he is preoccupied with this issue. For example, he recently asked me: "Can a Muslim practice modern financing techniques without compromising his core beliefs?" My answer was immediate: "Anwar, OGEL is not in the religion business! We are here to expand your country's economic base. We can do it expensively with a foreign crew, or we can train promising locals like you to do it more efficiently and in a more cost effective manner. The future of your country is at stake here. Do you think that the opinions of some old-fashioned religious leaders should dictate your country's well-being?" Needless to say, Anwar and I have not settled this discussion yet.

Still, Anwar is a likable fellow. Except for the time he takes off for prayers, he has been a conscientious employee. However, does he have what it takes to be an OGEL executive? Were it not for our delicate relations with the Malay government and their emphasis on Malayanization, I would have forced him to conform to OGEL's values and beliefs or asked him to leave. Unfortunately, any such firing is likely to attract the attention of the government and some of the more outspoken imams. They could easily turn public opinion against us, and we would have to cede our exploration rights here to other competitors. After all, look at what Algeria is doing to the French! OGEL cannot afford to make the government unhappy.

As I see it, we can deal with the Anwar Ahmad situation in any of the following ways:

- Delay the Malayanization program until we find trainees more enthusiastic about the OGEL culture and image, and promote these trainees over Anwar.
- Reshape the training program to include cultural factors (such as Islam), and redefine the job description of future Malay managers to include these factors.

- Gradually fire all Malay employees who refuse to participate in management training programs whatever their reason for not participating.
- Make it expensive for Malay employees not to accept management training. This can easily be done by offering substantial incentives for participating in training programs, i.e., expensive company cars, program completion bonuses, fast promotion after successful completion of training.

Which of the above would you recommend? Time is running short, and Anwar will be interviewed shortly for his willingness to participate in the next set of training programs."

Can You Pass this Job Test? [205]

Section A

1. What would you do if your young child came home with a shoplifted item?
   a. Take him back to the store.
   b. Give him a good talking to.
   c. Send him back to the store.
   d. None of the above.

Section B

	Yes	No
1. If you saw another person stealing on the job, would you turn that person in to the boss?		
2. Have you ever been disgusted with yourself because you did something dishonest?		
3. Is it very important for you to be trusted?		
4. Is stealing from one's job a common occurrence at this time?		
5. Have you ever been told, by a co-worker, how to cheat the company?		
6. Do you think people who steal do it because they always have?		
7. Joe always worked late without getting paid for it. Do you think it would be right for him to take his carfare from petty cash?		

Section C

	Yes	No
1. When you are wrong, do you usually admit it?		
2. Do you ever worry about what other people think of you?		
3. Did you ever cheat in school?		
4. Have you ever thought about cheating anyone out of anything?		
5. Did you ever lie to a teacher or a policeman?		
6. Have you ever stolen anything from an employer?		
7. Have you ever looked in a mirror and wished you could change something about yourself?		

Section D

	Yes	No
1. Are you always completely truthful about yourself?		

---

[205] From *Newsweek*, May 5, 1986. "Can You Pass This Job Test?"

2. Have you ever just thought of trying to steal something from anyplace?
3. Have you ever made a mistake on any of your jobs that cost your employer?

Section E

Yes No

1. Do you believe cheating people is not as bad as stealing money?
2. Have you ever wanted to be famous?
3. Do you think you are sometimes too honest?
4. Do you believe that everyone is dishonest to a certain degree?
5. Do you agree with the statement that "once a thief, always a thief"?

Ethics Role-Playing Exercise: The Adventures of Sāmī

Ḥasan is a junior customs clerk in Mauritius. He comes from a relatively poor family, and has overcome tremendous odds to attain his current position. He is an excellent worker, and has dreamed about advancing in rank to the position of supervisor. Promotion to this rank will require that he obtains the highest scores on the Civil Service examinations.

Several years ago, during high school, Ḥasan was working day and night in order to help his family. Sāmī, a classmate, used to help Ḥasan out by letting him borrow his books. He would even share his lunch with the starving Ḥasan. Since then, Sāmī and Ḥasan have become very good friends. Sāmī is from the same high school as Ḥasan, is an average customs clerk, and wants to become supervisor too. Unfortunately, with his work record and study habits, Sāmī is unlikely to obtain a high Civil Service examination score.

The exams are only two weeks away. Ḥasan is studying as hard as he can when he receives a visit from Sāmī. A senior government official in charge of the exams is willing to "tutor" junior customs clerk for a substantial fee. This official claims that previous clerks tutored by him have scored extremely high on the exam, and have subsequently been promoted to the rank of supervisor. Sāmī is already being tutored by this official. Because you are his friend, Sāmī wanted you to have the same opportunity.

Imagine that you are Ḥasan.

1. Should you accept Sāmī's offer and pay the official to be "tutored"? Yes____ No____. Why or why not?

____

____

____

2. Should you turn in the official to the police? Yes____ No____. Why or why not?

____

____

____

Index

—A—

—B—

—C—

—D—

—E—

IIIT English Publications

A. Islamization of Knowledge

0- B004 *Islamization of Knowledge: General Principles and Work Plan,* 3rd edition (1416/1995).

1- B008 *Toward an Islamic Theory of International Relations: New Directions for Methodology and Thought,* by 'AbdulḤamīd AbūSulaymān 2nd revised edition (1414/1993).

2- B010 *Toward Islamic Anthropology: Definitions, Dogma, and Directions* by Akbar Ṣ. Aḥmad (1406/1986).

3- B007 *Toward Islamic English* by Ismā'īl Rājī al Fārūqī (1406/1986).

4- B009 *Modelling Interest-Free Economy: A Study in Microeconomics and Development* by Muḥammad Anwar (1407/1987).

5- B014 *Islam: Source and Purpose of Knowledge.* Papers presented to the Second International Conference of Islamic Thought and the Islamization of Knowledge (1409/1988).

6- B016 *Toward Islamization of Disciplines.* Papers presented to the Third International Conference on Islamic Thought and the Islamization of Knowledge (1409/1988).

7- B012 *The Organization of the Islamic Conference: An Introduction to an Islamic Political Institution* by 'Abdullāh al Aḥsan (1408/1988).

8- B018 *Proceedings of the Lunar Calendar Conference.* Papers presented to the Conference of the Lunar Calendar. Edited by Imād ad-Dean Ahmad (1408/1988).

9- B020 *Islamization of Attitudes and Practices in Science and Technology.* Papers presented to a special seminar on the same topic. Edited by M.A.K. Lodhi (1409/1989).

10- B031 *Where East Meets West: The West on the Agenda of the Islamic Revival* by Mona Abul-Fadl (1412/1992).

11- B052 *Qur'anic Concept of Human Psyche.* Papers presented to a special seminar organizerd by IIIT Pakistan. Edited by Zafar Afaq Ansari (1412/1992).

12- B040 *Islam and the Economic Challenge* by M. Umer Chapra. Published jointly with the Islamic Foundation (U.K.) (1412/1992).

13- B041 *Resource Mobilization and Investment in an Islamic Economic Framework.* Papers presented to the 3rd International Islamic Economic Seminar. Edited by Zaidi Sattar (1412/1991).

14- B057 *Islam and Economic Development* by M. Umer Chapra. Published jointly with the Islamic Research Institute (Pakistan) (1413/1993).

15- B062 *An Introduction to Islamic Economics* by Muhammad Akram Khan. Published jointly with the Institute of Policy Studies (Pakistan) (1414/1994).

16- B044 *The Education Conference Book: Planning, Implementation, Recommendations and Abstracts of Papers.* Translated from Arabic and edited by Fathi Malkawi and Hussein Abdul-Fattah (1412/1992).

17- B080 *Contributions of Islamic Thought in Contemporary Economics.* Papers presented to the conference, jointly held by IIIT and Al Azhar University, Cairo, Egypt Edited by Misbah Oreibi. (Forthcoming, 1409/1988) .

B. Issues in Contemporary Islamic Thought

1- B001 *Trialogue of the Abrahamic Faiths,* Papers presented to the Islamic Studies Group of the American Academy of Religion. Edited by Ismā'īl Rājī al Fārūqī. 2nd edition (1406/1986).

2- B011 *Islamic Awakening: Between Rejection and Extremism* by Yūsuf al Qaraḍāwī. Published jointly with American Trust Publications, 2nd revised edition (1412/1992). Translated from Arabic.

3- *Madīnan Society at the Time of the Prophet,* by Akram Ḍiyā' al 'Umarī. Translated from Arabic.
B026 Volume I: *Its Characteristics and Organization* (1411/1991).
B027 Volume II: *The Jihad Against the Mushrikūn* (1411/1991).
B065 Both volumes in one book (1416/1995).

4- B002 *Tawḥīd: Its Implications for Thought and Life,* by Ismā'īl Rājī al Fārūqī 3rd edition (1416/1995).

5- B047 *Ethics of Disagreement in Islam,* by Ṭāhā Jābir al 'Awānī, 2nd edition (1417/1996).

7- B006 *Islamic Thought and Culture.* Papers presented to the Islamic Study Group of the American Academy of Religion. Edited by Ismā'īl Rājī al Fārūqī (1402/1982).

8- B003 *Essays in Islamic and Comparative Studies.* Papers presented to the Islaimc Study Group of the American Academy of Religion. Edited by Ismā'īl Rājī al Fārūqī (1402/1982).

9- B081 *Development of Religious Concepts in Muslim Children.* (Forthcoming).

10- B082 *How to Understand and Apply the Sunnah.* By Yūsuf al Qaraḍāwī. (Forthcoming).

11- B050 *Economic Growth and Human Resource Development in an Islamic Perspective.* Proceedings of the Fourth International Islamic Economics Seminar. Edited by Dr. Ehsan Ahmed (1413/1993).

12- B049 *Association of Muslim Social Scientists:* Proceeding of the Twenty First annual Conference. Edited by Muna Abul-Fadl (1413/1993).

13- B066 *Role of Private and Public Sectors in Economic Development in an Islamic Perspective.* Proceedings of the Fifth International Islamic Economics Seminar. Edited by Ehsan Ahmed (1416/1996).

C. Research Monographs

1- B023 *Source Methodology in Islamic Jurisprudence: (Uṣūl al Fiqh al Islāmī),* by Ṭāhā Jābir al 'Alwānī, 3rd edition (1413/1993). Translated from Arabic.

2- B022 *Islam and the Middle East: The Aesthetics of a Political Inquiry* by Mona Abul-Fadl (1411/1990).

3- B037 *Sources of Scientific Knowledge: The Concept of Mountains in the Qur'an* by Zaghloul R. El-Naggar (1411/1991).

4- B058 *Indexation of Financial Assets: An Islamic Evaluation* by S. M. Hasanuz Zaman (1413/1993).

5- B070 *The Making of a Religions Discourse: An Essay in the History and Historiography of the 'Abbāsid Revolution* by Muhammad Qasim Zaman (1415/1995).

D. Occasional Papers

1- B019 *Outlines of a Cultural Strategy* by Ṭāhā Jābir al 'Alwānī. French and German translations available (1410/1989). Translated from Arabic.

2- B035 *Islamization of Knowledge: A Methodology* by 'Imād al Dīn Khalīl. French translation available (1412/1991). Translated from Arabic.

3- B036 *The Qur'an and the Sunnah: The Time-Space Factor* by Ṭāhā Jābir al 'Alwānī and 'Imād al Dīn Khalīl. Translated from Arabic. French and German translations available (1412/1991).

4- B045 *Ijtihād* by Ṭāhā Jābir al 'Alwānī. Translated from Arabic. (1413/1993).

5- B055 *Laxity, Moderation and Extremism in Islam* by Aisha Lemu (1414/1994).

6- B059 *Islamization: Reforming Contemporary Knowledge* by 'AbdulḤamīd AbūSulaymān (1414/1994).

7- B061 *Toward Global Cultural Renewal: Modernity and the Episteme of Transcendence* by Mona Abul-Fadl (1416/1995).

8- B060 *The Islamization of Knowledge: Yesterday and Today* by Ṭāhā Jābir al 'Alwānī. Translated from Arabic. (1416/1995).

9- B079 *Missing Dimensions in Contemporary Islamic Movements* by Ṭāhā Jābir al 'Alwānī. Translated from Arabic. (1417/1996)

16- B053 *Knowledge: An Islamic Perspective* by Bakhtiar Ḥusain Siddiqui (1412/1991).

17- B046 *Islamization of Knowledge: A Critical Overview* by Sayyed Vali Reza Nasr (1413/1992).

E. Human Development

1- B030 *Training Guide for Islamic Workers* by Hisham Altalib, (third revised edition 1413/1993). French, Turkish, Malay, Urdu, Portugese and Arabic translations are available.

2- B083 *Islamic Business Ethics* by Rafik Issa Beekun (Forthcoming 1417/1997).

F. Perspectives on Islamic Thought

1- B024 *National Security and Development Strategy* by Arshad Zaman (1412/1991).

2- B054 *Nationalism and Internationalism in Liberalism, Marxism and Islam* by Tahir Amin (1412/1991).

3- B063 *Theories of Islamic Law: The Methodology of Ijtihad* by Imran Ahsan Khan Myazee (1416/1995).

G. Islamic Methodology

1- B048 *Crisis in the Muslim Mind* by 'AbdulḤamīd A. Abūsulaymān (1414/1993). Translated from Arabic.

H. Academic Dissertations

1- B051 *Through Muslim Eyes: M. Rashīd Riḍā and the West* by Emad Eldin Shaheen. 2nd edition (1415/1994).

2- B067 *Qur'anic Text: Toward a Methodology of Subject Indexing* by Hānī 'Aṭīyah (1417/1996).

3- B068 *Economic Doctrines of Islam: A Study in the Doctrines of Islam and Their Implications for Poverty, Employment and Economic Growth* by Irfan Ul Haq (1417/1996).

5- B071 *Business Ethics in Islam* by Mushtaq Ahmad (1416/1996).

7- B069 *Teachers Training: An Islamic Perspective* by Zafar Iqbal (1416/1996).

8- B084 *Social Justice in Islam* by Diena 'Abdul Qādir, (Fortcoming, 1417/1997).

7- B085 *The Variant Readings of the Qur'an: A Critical Study of Their Historical and Linguistic Origins* by Ahmad A. M. 'Abd Allah. (Forthcoming, 1417/1997).

7- B086 *Working Principles for an Islamic Model in Mass Communications*, by Suhaib al Barzinji. (Forthcoming, 1417/1997).

7- B087 *Addjudication in the Maliki Madhhab* by Mahammad Fadel. (Forthcoming 1417/1997).

I. Supplementary Social Studies Teaching Units

K- B072A *Kindergarten: I Am a Muslim: A Modern Storybook* by Susan Douglass.

1- B073A *First Grade: Eid Mubarak! Islamic Celebration Around the World* by Susan Douglass.

2- B074A *Second Grade: Muslims in Our Community & Around the World* by Susan Douglass.

3- B075A *Third Grade: Muslim Cities Then & Now* by Susan Douglass.

4- B076A *Fourth Grade: Introduction to Geography: Where in the World Do Muslims Live?* by Susan Douglass.

5- B077A *Fifth Grade: Traders & Explorers in Wooden Ships* by Susan Douglass.

6- B078A *Sixth Grade: Islam & Muslim Civilization* by Susan Douglass.

Journals

AJISS *American Journal of Islamic Social Sciences* (AJISS). A quarterly published jointly with the Association of Muslim Social Scientists (AMSS), U.S.A.

MWBR *Muslim World Book Review and Index of Islamic Literature.* A quarterly published jointly with the Islamic Foundation (U.K.).

Distributors of IIIT Publications

Belgium Secompex, Boulevard. Mourice Lemonnier, 152
1000 Bruxelles Tel: (32-2) 512-4473 Fax: (32-2) 512-8710

Egypt IIIT Office, 26-B Al Jazirah al Wusta St., Zamalek, Cairo
Tel: (202) 340-9520 Fax: (202) 340-9520

France Libraire Essalam, 135 Boulevard de Menilmontant 75011 Paris
Tel: (33-1) 4338-1956 Fax: (33-1) 4357-4431

Holland Rachad Export, Le Van Swindenstr. 108 II, 1093 Ck. Amsterdam
Tel: (31-20) 693-3735 Fax: (31-20) 693-882

India Genuine Publications & Media (Pvt.) Ltd., P.O. Box 9725, Jamia Nagar,
New Delhi 110 025 Tel: (91-11) 630-989 Fax: (91-11) 684-1104

Jordan IIIT Office, P.O. Box 9489, Amman
Tel: (962-6) 639-992 Fax: (962-6) 611-420

Lebanon Unite Arab Bureau, P.O. Box 135788, Beirut
Tel: (961-1) 807-779 Fax: (961-1) 804-257

Morocco *Dar al Aman* for Publishing and Distribution,
4 Zangat al Ma'muniyah, Rabat Tel: (212-7) 723-276 Fax: (212-7) 200-055

Saudi Arabia International Islamic Publishing House,
P.O. Box 55195, Riyadh 11534, Tel: (966-1) 1-465-0818 Fax: (966-1) 1-463-3489

United Arab Imirates Reading for All Bookshop, P.O. Box 11032 Dubai
Tel: (971-4) 663-903 Fax: (971-4) 690-084

United Kingdom

- Muslim Information Services, 233 Seven Sisters Rd.
  London N4 2DA Tel: (44-71) 272-5170 Fax: (44-71) 272-3214
- The Islamic Foundation, Markfield Da'wah Centre, Rutby Lane Markfield,
  Leicester LE6 ORN, U.K. Tel: (44-530) 244-944/45 Fax: (44-530) 244-946

U. S. A.

- amana Publications ,10710 Tucker Street, Beltsville MD, 20705-2223, USA
  Tel: (301) 595-5777 Fax: (301) 595-5888, E-mail: igfx@aol.com
- Islamic Book Service, 2622 East Main Street, Plainfield, IN 46168
  Tel: (317) 839-8150 Fax: (317) 839-2511
- Al Sa`dawi Publications, P.O. Box 4059, Alexandria, VA 22303 USA
  Tel: (703) 751-4800 Fax: (703) 751-4833